Blood

Blood begins amidst the horrific carnage of the In follows the journey of two young Sikhs from their small rural community in the Punjab to the Britain of the 1960's.

Blood was premièred at the Royal Court Theatre Upstairs on 24 August 1989.

HARWANT S. BAINS was Thames TV Writer in Residence at the Royal Court in 1988 and his first play **The Flying Kite** was performed at the Theatre Royal Stratford East in 1987. He is currently writing a film for Channel 4.

Methuen New Theatrescripts series offers frontline intelligence of the most original and exciting work from the fringe.

authors in the same series

Karim Alrawi
Thomas Babe
Aphra Behn
Edward Bond
Howard Brenton
Mikhail Bulgakov
Edward Bulwer-Lytton
Bob Carlton
Jim Cartwright
Caryl Churchill
Tony Craze, Ron Hart,
Johnnie Quarrell
Sarah Daniels
Nick Darke
Nick Dear
David Edgar
Harvey Fierstein
Peter Flannery
Peter Gibbs
Andre Gregory
Robert Holman
Debbie Horsfield
Dusty Hughes
Ron Hutchinson
Tunde Ikoli
Terry Johnson
Charlotte Keatley
Manfred Karge
Barrie Keeffe
Paul Kember
Thomas Kilroy
Hanif Kureishi
David Lan
Deborah Levy
Kate Lock
Stephen Lowe
Doug Lucie
John Mackendrick

David Mamet
Tony Marchant
Philip Massinger
Mustapha Matura
Michael Meyer
Anthony Minghella
Adrian Mitchell
Tom Murphy
G F Newman
Louise Page
Harold Pinter
Stephen Poliakoff
Christina Reid
David Rudkin
William Saroyan
Ntozake Shange
Wallace Shawn
C P Taylor
Sue Townsend
Michelene Wandor & Mike
Alfreds
Timberlake Wertenbaker
Peter Whelan
Michael Wilcox
Nigel Williams
Snoo Wilson
Charles Wood
Nicholas Wright

Blood

A Play by

Harwant S. Bains

Methuen Drama

A Methuen New Theatrescript

First published as a paperback original in 1989 by Methuen Drama, Michelin House, 81 Fulham Road, London SW3 6RB and distributed in the United States of America by HEB Inc., 70 Court Street, Portsmouth, New Hampshire 03801

The photograph on the front cover is © Henri Cartier Bresson.

A CIP catalogue record for this book is available from the British Library

Printed in Great Britain by Expression Printers Ltd, London N7

Preface

Any work of the imagination must, I suppose, have its genesis in some obscure location deep beneath the layers of the conscious self. However, I think I can say that **Blood** was in some measure born of the desire to open a dialogue with a previous generation: that is, those men and women who cut away their roots to journey across the world and build what they hoped might be a better life. My generation, the 'second generation' as we are sometimes known, can never fully appreciate the courage that our mothers and fathers must have possessed to take the risks they did. They were adventurers of the first order, and we should not forget that.

The play is rooted within the specific world of Punjabi Sikhs. They are a people with their own proud – and bloody – history. Many of the elements employed within it were drawn from my own experiences as a part of this community. In some respects it is a very personal statement – I would not pretend for a moment that it deals with a 'normal' or 'commonplace' set of circumstances. But I have attempted, in my own way, to capture some truths about the world of which I am a part.

Yet **Blood** is in no sense a 'sociological' play. Its characters might be recognisable to some, but it would be a grave error to read it as a text concerning itself with explaining a 'community' or a 'culture'. There are other, far better mediums within which that can be attempted.

The generation to which my mother and father belong regards itself, in its darker moments, as somehow wasted. Men and women that could have achieved so much, were worthy of so much, who were instead ground down by the brutal demands of the 'host' Nation. My hope for the future is that the potential of subsequent generations – their children and grandchildren – will be better realised and embraced. As a writer, I know that there is a rich landscape laid out before me which I might to some extent explore. I hope that **Blood** is a step in the right direction.

Only in the conduct of our action can we find the sense of mastery over of the Fates.

Joseph Conrad **Nostromo**

Da is freilich das Blut.
Das Blut ist das Schwertse. Das Blut ist schewer.

(Of course, there's blood.
Blood is the hardest. Hard as stone.)

Rainer Maria Rilke **Das Lied Des Idioten (The Idiot's Song)** trans. Stephen Mitchell

For Carolyn, Michael H and G.P.D.

Blood was first performed at the Royal Court Theatre Upstairs on 24 August 1989, with the following cast:

BALBIR/BALBIR'S FATHER	Paul Bhattacharjee
INDIAN WORKER/THIRD MAN	Bhasker
YOUNG MANMOHAN	Sean Ramnath-O'Neill
THE INDIAN PRIME MINISTER/SECOND MAN	Kulvinder Ghir
JANE	Debra Gillett
YOUNG BALBIR	Ronak Manek
MANMOHAN	Dev Sagoo
SURINDER	Meera Syal
HARJEET/FIRST MAN	Gordon Warnocke
POLISH LANDLORD/WHITE WORKER/BODYGUARD	Jimmy Yuill

Directed by Lindsay Posner
Designed by Julian McGowan
Lighting by Tina MacHugh
Music by Stephen Warbeck

Brief Description of the Set

Four pillars arranged in a semi-circle, upon these is suspended a semi-circular ramp which will serve as a second playing area. Beyond the pillars the constellations vaguely depicted against total blackness. The pillars and ramp should appear to be made of marble. The suggestion to the audience might initially be that we are in some sort of temple or mausoleum. The theatrical 'reality' of the interior scenes will be in direct contrast to the wider environment which encircles the action of the play.

(Note. This was not the set used for the Royal Court Theatre Upstairs production. However, it was the type of structure that I had in mind when writing the play, and thus may be of assistance to the reader.)

Act One

Scene 1

An empty stage, the lights fully up. Blood begins to trickle down each of the four pillars. As this happens: music – the 'Flower Song' from Act one of Lakme by Delibes. This music should 'bleed' in and out of the first scene. We watch for a few moments, then . . . Gradual darkness. Dim lights, growing gradually brighter with the reflected light of burning buildings.

India, 1947. The time of partition. There is a backcloth upon which the fiery reflection of burning buildings is projected. A tattered and burned Indian flag falls and hangs limply in the background to dominate the area beneath the platform.

The sounds of riot. Chanting, screaming, shouting. **Balbir's Father** *runs on from stage left pulling the young* **Balbir** *along with him, he carries a long wooden stick which has been made into an improvized spear. Being unable to run any further, he stops and turns to face the men pursuing him.* **First Man** *enters running carrying a scythe and a burning torch, his clothes spattered with blood. He is closely followed by a* **Second Man** *who is carrying a long home-made spear and has a blood-stained dagger tucked into a belt around his waist.* **Balbir's Father** *uses his spear to hold them back.*

After a few moments a **Third Man** *enters dragging the mutilated body of a woman behind him. All three men are dressed in an eclectic fashion, as if they have been picking items of clothing off diverse individuals. It is important that this scene should be played in an almost wistful manner, the temptation to over-dramatize should be avoided at all costs.*

First Man *(smiling)* Nowhere to run to is there mister?

Third Man *(crouching over the body)* She's still warm.

First Man You're a big bloke aren't ya? (*To* **Second Man**.) I'n'e big, ey?

Over this the **Third Man** *has tied a cord around the woman's neck, he strangles her.* **Balbir's Father** *tries to run forward to stop him. The* **First Man** *bars his way.*

Balbir's Father Rani!

First Man What'll you do now? Life is cheap friend.

Third Man She's nice and sweaty, come on. (*He pulls up his Dhoti and parts the legs of the corpse.*) My turn first though, I'll do the honours.

Second Man What you doin'?

Third Man Fucking.

First Man (*to* **Balbir's Father**) Come on wanker, let's end it. (**Balbir** – *who is clinging to his father in terror – screams. His* **Father** *calms him by stroking his hair.*) 'E's a nice boy. Nice boy. (*To* **Second Man**.) What you reckon?

Second Man I'm for a bit.

First Man I bet you is. (*Seeing* **Third Man**, *who is busy fornicating with the corpse.*) Who said the age of romance is dead eh? 'E was a wise man.

Third Man This is so good.

Second Man Let's get goin' maybe.

First Man Hear that? Your missus is a good fuck mister.

With a shout **Balbir's Father** *lunges forward.* **First Man** *runs backward and falls over.* **Second Man** *runs forward. Thinking of his son,* **Balbir's Father** *retreats.* **First Man** *gets up.*

Don't get so angry. What quarrel 'ave we got eh? Us, we're jus' goin along with the way things are innit. The world's a fucking nuthouse.

Suddenly a cry of victory goes up in the distance as there is an explosion.

Second Man They done it, they got the mosque. (*To* **Third Man**.) You're takin' your time.

Third Man I'm gonna make me a dead child.

The **Third Man** *starts to orgasm. He is holding a knife with both hands across the head of the corpse, and in his ecstasy decapitates it. Over the next speech he gets up and picks up the head, examining it with fascination. He may also give it a gentle kiss on the lips.*

First Man I'm a butcher, that's my . . . pro-fession! I wield my steel with expertise an' skill. Can't remember my faith, my religious persuasion. No, I cannot remember. Gimme the boy!

Balbir's Father No! Never!

First Man I'm a protector of little children. I'll make him well . . . make him happy. Just give 'im, you can go.

Balbir's Father I'll kill you. Just try and I'll kill you.

First Man It's three on one, friend.

Balbir's Father (*moving* **Balbir** *so that he is protected by his own body*) I'll die killing you. But you will die too my friend. You will die.

Second Man Come on!

Third Man Catch! (*Throwing the head to* **Second Man**, *who catches it and impales it on the end of his spear.*) . . . Who's next? I've got 'er well opened up.

Second Man Is that a smile on 'er face?

Balbir's Father (*shielding* **Balbir's** *eyes from what is going on*) Oh my God, let this end, oh my God.

First Man What does it matter anymore? We're just here running round with no reasons in our pockets. What you reckon, what are we, which way're we travellin'? Which border we aiming to cross? God knows! (*Looking up at the sky.*) The Gods! Oh they're wanking off at the sight of this, they're lovin' it! You a religious man?

Balbir's Father Yes.

First Man I can tell. You look like an abandoned puppy.

Second Man Le'ss 'ave the boy.

Third Man Oh yes. Very nice. Afters as well, ey? (*He laughs at his witticism.*)

Balbir's Father Let him go. Please.

First Man Yeah?

Balbir's Father I'll stay. Let him go.

First Man But you're not as sweet.

Balbir's Father Let him go. I will stay. Otherwise I will first kill my son, then you.

Third Man (*turning*) Smell that!

Second Man Flesh.

Third Man What a stink.

First Man O.K. He can go.

Second Man You what!?

First Man (*he goes up to the* **Second Man**, *winks at him, then takes his knife.*) He can go. On condition.

Balbir's Father What condition?

First Man (*holding up the dagger*) See this? I give this to you see. You take it. You sacrifice yourself to the life of your boy. That's it. You put this into your heart and the boy runs free an' happy.

Balbir's Father Let him go first.

Balbir No dad!

First Man No dad!

Balbir's Father Let him go first, then I give you your wish.

First Man Alright.

Third Man This'll be something t' see.

Second Man I'd prefer we try for the boy.

First Man (*to* **Balbir**) Go on kiddie.

Balbir's Father *kisses him, then pushes him to run.*

Balbir (*refusing to go*) Dad! Dad!

Balbir's Father Go on. I love you. Go on.

First Man Go on, he loves you.

Balbir *runs, but then stops out of his father's eyeshot to watch. In the meantime,* **First Man** *has thrown the dagger onto the ground in front of* **Balbir's Father.**

Deal's a deal.

Balbir's Father *slowly bends to pick up the dagger. At the same time he puts down the spear.*

Well now.

Second Man Lost yer guts? We'll ave t' do it.

First Man (*waving him back*) Wait!

Balbir's Father *puts the knife to his chest. A pause. The men look on with growing excitement.*

First Man Yes! Yes!

Balbir's Father *plunges the knife into his chest. He stands holding it in.*

Balbir's Father Balbir, mera piara!

Balbir Dad!

He runs back towards his father. At the same time there is a volley of rifle fire nearby.

Second Man Come on!

Third Man It's the army! Must be!

Second Man (*to* **First Man***, who is watching* **Balbir** *run to his father with a smile on his face*) Come on now, come on.

First Man No, hold on.

Third Man *runs off.*

Second Man There'll be others, loads.

First Man Will there?

Second Man We'll head for Jullundur, then on to Amritsar. The whole Punjab is in flames they say. The whole bloody Country.

First Man (*serenely*) The whole Universe maybe eh? What can we do?

He puts his arm around the **Second Man***, they hug in a brotherly manner. Short pause, then* **Second Man** *runs off. Going over to where* **Balbir** *is crying over his father, he bends down to undo his hair knot and release the long hair. He speaks with a gentle sing-song voice.*

Me I had a boy like you. He was a prince among songs. (*He runs the scythe gently along the length of* **Balbir's** *body.*) I'm gonna cut you open frontways. Then I'm gonna turn you and cut you from skull to arsehole. I'm gonna rip you in two. Then I'm gonna scoop you out, scoop out your insides and smear them over me face while I chew on yer eyeballs! (*The* **Man** *raises the scythe to chop at* **Balbir***. There is a scream from nearby and the man looks around. He holds* **Balbir** *by his long hair.*) Listen! Can't tell if it's woman or man, human or animal, there's no more distinctions!

Balbir *manages to shove him away, in the ensuing struggle he knees him in the testicles. The* **Man** *gives a shout and falls off him – dropping the scythe.* **Balbir** *makes to run off stage right, but then seeing the scythe he picks it up and runs back to where the man lies clutching at his genitals.*

What's yer name? Tell me, tell me yer name!

Balbir (*sobbing*) Balbir Singh. You're fucked now.

First Man Yes, yes. Go on! Go on Balbir Singh!

Suddenly he lunges. **Balbir** *brings the scythe down cutting into him. A scream and blackout. The screams and sounds of a riot intensify and then fade.*

Scene 2

India. Circa 1948.

Two young boys, **Manmohan** *and* **Balbir** *sit in a sun-bleached and recently harvested field.* **Balbir** *is chewing a sugar cane, while* **Manmohan** *lies back looking up into the sky. The boys are about eleven to twelve years old. Each of them has a rag wrapped around his right hand.*

Manmohan It's such a big sky.

Balbir *looks up.*

You get dizzy like this, looking up. Everything spins around after a bit.

Balbir Don't look up then.

Manmohan I don't want the rains to come.

Balbir They have to come. For the crops.

Manmohan I know. (*Sitting up.*) But I still like the sun best, with the clear skies.

Balbir Sun turns you black. Makes your face like a bumhole. Makes you stink of piss.

Manmohan Look at these fields, I walked them yesterday, all over. Took me a whole two hours – an' I wasn't going slow. We'll have to work them when we're like dad, when we're big . . . the both of us.

Pause.

Balbir Your dad and the three brothers were arguing last night.

Manmohan (*gently emphasizing a point*)

Our dad . . . how do you know?

Balbir I went out in the verandah, I could hear them. They want to slice up dad's land and take a share. They said they'd get him with the law. Dad got so angry. He said no way, never. He told them go jump in a well.

Manmohan It's not fair, why do they want ours when they got their own?

Balbir It's what your grandad left, the way he shared it out. They say they got the shit earth. It's cos they're black-hearted bastards.

Manmohan They've always been nice to me. They make us toys and play with us don't they?

Balbir Tha'ss jus' t' make us think they're nice. I'm only sayin' what dad was sayin'. I'm jus' tellin' you.

Manmohan Dad wont let them . . . I'm going to say to him . . . it's not for the three brothers it's for us . . . Dad's strong, he won't let them.

Balbir You'll be in shit if he loses to 'em You'll have sod all then. (*Short pause.*) You wanna make a game? Something with running and wrestling in it.

Manmohan (*after a short pause*)   Mr Chatterjee will miss us soon. It's his lesson now.

Balbir He won't. He's a blind bat. He only ever sees the blackboard.

Manmohan One of the boys might tell him.

Balbir I'd beat shit out of anyone who did.

Manmohan Would you?

Balbir Yes.

Pause.

Manmohan We could go and swim in the river if you want.

Balbir I want to plant something to grow first.

Manmohan Plant something?

Balbir This ground's perfect.

Manmohan What could we grow?

Balbir Lots of things . . . Money.

Manmohan Money? You can't grow money, it's paper and metal.

Balbir You think I'm a liar then?

Manmohan No . . . but you can't.

Balbir Anything grows in the right ground.

Manmohan Even money?

Balbir If you give it time.

Manmohan I've never heard that before.

Balbir That's because they don't tell people, else everyone would be rich. Only some people know.

Manmohan How do you know then?

Balbir I found out.

Manmohan How?

Balbir That's a holy secret.

Manmohan Even from me?

Balbir How do I know you won't go and tell everyone.

Pause. **Manmohan** *unwinds the bandage from his hand and shows his bloody hand to* **Balbir.**

You don't believe it though. What's the point telling you?

Manmohan Would you tell me if I believed you?

Balbir You'd have to really believe.

Manmohan Really believe?

Balbir Inside your heart.

Pause. **Manmohan** *takes out a rupee note and gives it to* **Balbir.**

Manmohan You could plant this.

Balbir (*unfolding the note carefully*) I wondered where you hid it.

Manmohan I didn't hide it. I was keeping it to save. (**Balbir** *digs a little hole and puts the note into it.*) Will you tell me now?

Short pause.

Balbir I'll tell you at the river.

Manmohan Why not here?

Balbir The river's a better place for telling things. (*Getting up.*) Race you there!

Manmohan (*getting up*) You always win me!

Balbir Alright, head start . . . go on!

Manmohan *dashes off.* **Balbir** *feigns the beginning of a run, but quickly doubles back and digs up the note. As he does this two men in grey suits carrying luggage come on stage left and stand by a pillar. They look up at the sky. These are the adult* **Balbir** *and* **Manmohan.** *The lights darken slightly.* **Balbir,** *now sitting cleaning the soles of his bare feet, looks at the men.*

What're you lookin' at? In the village they go on about how the soil is our saviour. Those people have got shit fer brains. They live and die in the middle of nowhere. (*Seeing an ant by his foot he crushes it.*) They live like insects. They can stuff their bloody land for all I care.

He runs off after **Manmohan.**

Scene 3

As the lights go down on the previous scene, a spotlight comes up on **Balbir** *and* **Manmohan** *(as adults – still by the pillar). The sound of a large passenger airliner passing overhead. We are in Heathrow Airport, 1960.* **Manmohan** *and* **Balbir** *carry* *two large suitcases each. They also have a 'razai' (quilt) under their arms.*

Manmohan (*putting down his luggage. With pain in his voice*) Oh shit.

Balbir What? What now?

Manmohan Look at this place.

Balbir (*putting down his cases*) We're not here to see the sights.

Manmohan So many white people.

Balbir What bloody colour did you expect them to be?

Manmohan But not like this . . . grey . . . Especially the ladies. Many of them look dead.

Balbir Many of them probably are. Now come on.

Manmohan Have you got the address? (**Balbir** *takes a scrap of paper from his breast pocket.*) How will we find it yaar?

Balbir We'll take a taxi. Jaswant said in his letter that this Shepherds Bush place is a few miles from the airport. Don't be like a mouse all the time Manmohan!

He picks up his cases and walks on. The spotlight fades on **Manmohan** *looking up into the sky with a frightened expression on his face.*

Scene 4

Shepherds Bush, winter 1960. A double-sized room which looks out over railway tracks. Trains often pass by. The room is poorly decorated, and is furnished only with a double bed to stage right, a wardrobe and set of drawers against one wall, a table to the centre of the room. The floor is bare boards, except for the central area, which is covered with an off-cut of carpet. On one wall is a Coronation photograph of the Queen. There is also a wooden crucifix and a cheaply framed painting of the virgin Mary with a rosary dangling from it.

The single window faces the audience – the curtains drawn. Beneath the window there is fixed a gas fire above which there is a mantlepiece (upon which – amongst other things – is an old teacup). The one door to the room is to stage left. Enter the **Landlord**. *He is followed by* **Balbir** *and* **Manmohan**, *carrying some of their luggage.*

Landlord (*rubbing his hands together – it is a cold day. He speaks with a Polish accent*) Bit musty, az not been given air in long while. Take a look, take good look, this is it . . . (**Balbir** *sets the quilt down.*) I get bit more light in for you. (*The* **Landlord** *goes to the window and draws the curtains.*) Take it or leave, makes no difference. I prefers without lodgers but it is the wife . . . it is her instigation.

Balbir This country is so cold . . . Even inside. It is exceptional.

Landlord (*to* **Manmohan**) Make yourself comfy my friend. (**Manmohan** *goes and sits on one of the beds.*) That is the heater. Has not worked since wife's mother died in that exact very bed.

Manmohan *springs off the bed.* **Balbir** *and the* **Landlord** *both look at him. Embarrassment. Then, pretending that he had gotten up to check for something he might have lost,* **Manmohan** *pulls a suitcase key from his trouser pocket and holds it up with a smile.*

She lie stone cold, stone cold for three day before we notice. She was very private person. Heats is your responsibility. That is usual condition. I supply light. Cooking only at certain times specified. She will not share kitchen with foreigners originating from other countries you see. . . . Well?

Balbir (*shivering*) Yes. yes, thank you. (*Weakly.*) The room looks . . . homely.

Landlord Is 'homely' for two. Jus' the two is alright. No more. I vant no trouble. Just you.

Balbir Myself and Manmohan, my brother. No more.

Landlord What about the other one who come before . . . say he need room.

Balbir He was a schoolday friend, we asked him by letter to find us a place to stay.

Landlord Just don't vant no hanky panky or tricky business. I have experience of the oriental mind.

Balbir I must fetch the luggage. The taxi fellow is waiting.

Landlord Deposit first, then luggage. (**Balbir** *looks at him.*) One month in advance. Made all clear to your 'schoolday friend' in Queen's perfect English. One month in advance non-returnable. We shook the hands on this matter. (*Clenching his fist.*) Sealed in iron!

Balbir I thought that he had paid you, sir.

Landlord He only pay retainer. He not pay deposit. You want room you pay cash on barrel my bonnie brown friend.

Balbir (*searching his pockets*) Yes . . . yes . . . money, we do have, ik skint . . . one moment . . . My wallet – it is in my big coat.

He goes out. Pause.

Landlord (*to* **Manmohan**) You know jokes? Know any good jokes?

Manmohan Only in Punjabi sir.

Landlord What bloody use of that? I know twenty three dirty joke, all different. I know some give you biggest hard-on you ever have. Split your trouser. You wanna hear?

Manmohan *nods a reluctant 'yes', but at that moment* **Balbir** *returns with a suitcase and his overcoat.*

Manmohan Paise hageh ah?

Balbir Dekhthe kine mungtha.

Landlord I don't want no lingo . . . none of the hindoo stani business under this roof.

Balbir It is Punjabi sir.

Landlord What bloody difference!? I got certain principles. I'm a patriot. (*Pointing to the Virgin Mary.*) The pope is boss in this house, what he say goes. That's explanation vy I got so many bloody kids. Principles. (*He has a thought.*) The picture and the cross stays. You take it down, you out. Yes?

Balbir Yes. Of course. I have the money.

Landlord Good, because money is the key to self-advancement my friend. Now, you pay one month in advance . . . means twelve quids now plus one week's rent on top . . . fifteen quids in all.

Balbir But . . .

Landlord Is three quids a week.

Balbir It is all the money I have sir.

Landlord (*angrily*) Is that my fault? You want me to rot this floor with tears of sorrow? No sir! This heart in here is built of stone. You're lucky I takin' you in. Most round here say no vay to wogs or coons. No offence, but wogs or coons is not popular for the takin' in. Me I'm liberal minded. Now you wanna wear out good shoes looking elsewhere, is a free country we fight to establish.

Pause. **Balbir** *extracts some money and counts out fifteen pounds into the* **Landlord**'s *palm.*

There. Now I vant no monkey business, no wimmin', we all good Christians. (*Pause. The* **Landlord** *looks at the two men then hands* **Balbir** *back one pound.*) You will need food. Men suffering from starvation do not make good tenants.

Balbir We shall be model tenants. We shall be exceptional.

Manmohan *nods in agreement.*

You will be so happy sir!

Landlord I was a pilot in war, of fighter planes, Spitfires, 'Urricanes . . . flew zem all, dropped bombs on Hitler. I am not a man to mess with. I have eyes like vulture and ears like cat. I am cousin brother to Bela Lugosi. Ve take no shit.

Balbir We will be totally respectful, sir.

Landlord Right. (*Short pause.*) Place will need a clean out. (*He looks around.*) Right . . . right . . . You can have keys downstairs. (*He goes and stands at the door. He hesitates, then looks at his two tenants curiously.*) You've come a long way.

Balbir Yes, sir. A very long way. (*Pause. Looking out of the window.*) There is a railway outside.

Landlord White City tube is just down the road.

Balbir You hear Manmohan, we are in the White City!

Manmohan *does not seem pleased. He goes over to the window to look.*

Landlord For sightseeing you take the central line – right up the dirty bum of London. What you gonna do here? (*Pause.*) In this country, what is your plan of action?

Balbir We will work, sir.

Landlord You come to work?

Balbir To make a future.

Manmohan We have to send money for our farm.

Landlord I work best part of my life here. I fought Germans in war, then fought bosses in factory. Much the same thing. What it all for? For a woman who gets fatter and more wart-ridden by the day, and for kids who will piss on my grave. Well, I say good luck and good riddance to you. (*Short pause.*) The

factory is different to the farm. They will treat you like dogs. Be ready to be dogs.

Balbir Oh we'll be good barking dogs sir! Show us your bark Manmohan.

Manmohan *looks down shyly.* **Balbir** *goes over and pats him hard.*

Manmohan (*sulkily*) Woof.

Balbir You see, sir – well trained!

Landlord Very good! (*He looks at them both curiously for a moment.*) As long as there is mutual respect there will be no war between us, eh. (*He exits.*)

Manmohan Did you smell the fish?

Balbir It was him. Fat men are always smelly.

Manmohan (*rubbing himself*) It's so cold Balbir.

Balbir It is a cold country. (*He starts to unpack a suitcase.*) We'll go and look around. See what the place is like.

Manmohan You want to go out?

Balbir Yes.

Manmohan Now?

Balbir Why not yaar?

Manmohan I'll stay here.

Balbir (*throwing a blanket to him*) Here!

Manmohan My eyes and jaws are hurting. (*Rubbing his hands.*) My fingers . . . (*Going and sitting down on the bed.*) I will die very very soon.

Balbir Oh-ho, shut your gob please Manmohan. You are a total softy-softy.

Manmohan And also I'm hungry.

Balbir I'll find us food. We have one pound.

Manmohan How much is one pound?

Balbir Not enough.

Manmohan Don't go out tonight Balbir.

Balbir But you want food. And I want to explore.

Manmohan I will explore with you tomorrow. Please don't go yaar. He might come back.

Balbir (*going over to him and putting his arm around him*) O.K. brother, we'll starve tonight. We'll cuddle up and hide away from the mad, angry world. Then tomorrow we'll go and visit our friends. They'll take us to the big factory and get us wonderful jobs. Very soon we'll be rich men yaar. We'll have pound notes stuffed in our pockets, gold teeth and rings, and meat on our plates every single night. (*Pause.*) Manmohan?

Manmohan Nothing . . . just tiredness. Mummy was so sad at the station.

Balbir It's a mother's way.

Manmohan She cried for us both.

Balbir But mainly for her only son.

Manmohan You are a son to her also Balbir.

Pause. **Balbir** *gets up from the bed.*

Balbir Do you remember my mother Manmohan?

Manmohan Aunty had the kindest face. Everyone called her 'nice aunty'.

Balbir I can only remember tears yaar. And the strength of my daddy's arms.

Manmohan Don't bring back those times Balbir.

Balbir They're the shadows of my thoughts. (*Pause.*) The blood of my father.

Manmohan (*holding him*) Balbir . . . Balbir.

Balbir No three brothers will ever tear up our rightful soil.

Manmohan How long will we be in this place?

Balbir As long as lawyers have to be paid.

Manmohan To save our land, we have to leave our it far behind. Can that be right?

Pause.

Balbir Look, look. (*Going to the window.*) A field ripe for the planting. We'll bury our seeds and watch them flower. It's an adventure!

Manmohan Adventure?

Balbir Listen yaar, we are not men any longer. (*He spreads his arms out at ninety degrees to his body.*) We are telegraph poles . . . through us the wealth of this fine fertile land will be sent in little dot-dash-dot messages back to the village.

Manmohan In my first letter I will say, mummy, daddy, we are all fine and have found jobs, however Balbir has turned into a telegraph pole.

Balbir (*laughing*) Yes, tell them!

Manmohan I only want simple things. I only want my wife and a farm to work..

Balbir You will have much much more! (**Manmohan** *shakes his head.*) People have seen wonders here yaar – you've read the letters that come to the village.

Manmohan *puts his hands into his jacket pockets. He extracts two handfuls of soil and shows them to* **Balbir**. **Balbir** *goes over to him, he laughs.*

Balbir I thought you had sweets in there, Burfii.

Manmohan It's our field.

Balbir *touches it.*

Balbir Yes. It is.

He goes and fetches an old teacup which lies

on the mantle piece over the gas fire.
Manmohan *carefully pours in the soil.*
Balbir *takes the cup and looks into it.*

Balbir When we were kids, you
remember what we used to say? (*Pause.*)
Our oath.

Manmohan If this was the last drop of
water in my mouth, the last drop of
blood in my body . . .

Balbir I'd take it out and give it to you.
(*Going and putting the cup on the mantle
piece.*) We said silly things under the sun.

Pause. **Balbir** *walks upstage left, while*
Manmohan *walks to the diametrically
opposite position downstage right, he is in the
'corner' of the room and turns his face in
towards the wall.*

Balbir This is what I saw lying under the
sun with my eyes closed and the stink of
fresh cowpat in my nostrils. A strange
grey land with a crust of concrete over
the soil. A world without howling ghosts
roaming its surface.

Manmohan Why will I only ever speak in
whispers? I'll be loyal. Yes. Forever. But
where will I find the dreams we had?
Our lives are inscribed into thousands
of years in a place where our ancestors
fought to build their paradise – and
for us every other place is a land of the
dead.

Balbir Good and bad. No. Fresh cowpat
won't smell too good when you first
smell it. But it won't smell bad either.
Money doesn't smell good in used notes
some say . . . me I like that stench.
They've done their job, and they've got
real sweat clinging to the faces on them.

Scene 5

Platform, stage right. **Second** *and* **Third
Man** *enter, they are lost. The* **Second Man**
still carries the spear upon which is impaled

the now decomposing head. The **Third Man**
sits down on the ground exhausted.

Third Man No more. No way.

Second Man Keep moving, come on.
There's no hope otherwise. We'll be
stuck.

Third Man I wasn't born to this type of
activity. My legs are giving out. Maybe if
you gave them a rub.

Second Man What!?

Third Man Oh, look at the blisters I got!
A little rub. Just t'ease the cramps. My
wife always used to.

Second Man (*kneeling down*) Was she a
good woman? Was she pretty? (*He rubs
his legs gently.*)

Third man In her own strange way.
That's what my father said when he
organized the hitch-up. He had a fine
sense of the macabre.

Second Man Come on. We've got to
move on. We're not safe in the open.

Third Man Who cares?

Second Man Your mother. We're bound
to hit a village or town soon.

Third Man Then what? We mix in with
some local mob. I'm getting tired of all
the running around. What're we fighting
about? Someone really should say else it
gets hard t' keep up the enthusiasm.

Second Man Maybe yer right. Let's find
us a reason worth looking for. (*Squatting
down.*) Were you ever a killer before?

Third Man You what?

Second Man Were you?

Third Man I was good an' respectable.
Never thought myself above the law. But
laws are dead now.

Second Man We'll revert. We will. We'll
be family men again. It fascinates me the
way a million men can turn.

Third Man You make of life what you can, don't you? Make the best of it.

Second Man It's like . . . there's no true ground to stand on that won't shift. Like you can feel the earth is turning that bit more fast. Oh we got to head West. West is the way.

Third Man For what?

Second Man Out of the Punjab. Put it all behind us. The borders.

Third Man Fuck the borders. They'll be our nooses.

Second Man We'll slip away. There'll be new land, fresh. Too much death runs in this soil now. Crops will grow and wilt in the tears of orphans and widows.

Third Man Means sod all t'me. I'm no farmer. My family rose into government service.

Second Man Alright, pen pusher. You go find yourself another stiff t' screw. Me, I'm off.

Third Man Look wait, don't leave me. (*Rubbing his ankle.*) I think there's a sprain.

Second Man Well you're fuck all use t'me then.

Third Man Go a bit slow. I'll watch yer back.

The **Second Man** *pulls his companion up off the ground.*

Second Man Come on. We'll journey like brothers eh? We'll devise stories t' tell our kids.

Third Man My kids are dead.

Second Man You'll have others.

Scene 6

Night, the room. Dim lights gradually go up to show **Balbir** *illuminated only by a candle on*

the table. He is standing at the window looking out at heavy rain. **Balbir** *is wearing only his 'kucha' (shorts) and a vest. From his side hangs the small ceremonial dagger always carried by Sikhs. His turban lies on the table next to the candle. He takes a swig from a bottle of whiskey.*

Gradually the lights also go up on platform stage right. A large red setting sun in the background, casting its light over a desert. The **Second Man** *stands looking down towards* **Balbir**, *he holds the spear upon which the head is still impaled. The* **Third Man** *lies sleeping on the ground a little way behind him.*

Second Man The cracks in the land will turn to pools now. The peasants will dance in the first monsoon shower. They say the world is a curving mirror. (*Pause.*) What will happen, Balbir, when time dissolves? (*He raises his clenched hand to a ninety degree angle. A stream of sand falls slowly from his fingers.*) The sun will fade and leave us blind. The stars and planets will subside, just like us.

Lights on platform right fade, though the red disk representing the sun should remain faintly illuminated. **Balbir** *turns from the window and goes to sit at the table. He continues to drink from the whiskey bottle. After a short while* **Manmohan** *enters. Seeing the darkness he reaches out to switch on the electric light.*

Balbir No. Leave it off.

Manmohan *obeys. He closes the door and starts to take off his coat. Short pause.* **Manmohan** *sits down on his bed.*

Balbir Look at us. Miserable men. We go down on all fours in their factory like dumb creatures and in return they throw us some crumbs. Is this what we want for our lives? Is it all we deserve?

Manmohan It is . . . temporary. When we have sent back enough . . .

Balbir Enough? How much is that

Manmohan? We bleed ourselves dry to feed them. They've never had it so good. But what about our hunger?

Pause.

Manmohan The managers were asking why you didn't come in for your shift.

Balbir My shift?

Manmohan Your shift tonight. They were asking.

Balbir Were they?

Manmohan Yes . . . John.

Balbir John?

Manmohan John asked me.

Balbir He asked you?

Manmohan I told him you must be sick.

Balbir Sick?

Pause.

Manmohan Are you sick, Balbir?

Pause.

Are you sick?

Balbir Maybe I am.

Manmohan He gave me your wages. (*He takes out a packet.*)

Balbir Were you happy? Did that make you smile? Did you show him your teeth when you smiled? Did your mouth water?

Manmohan *takes the packet over to where* **Balbir** *is sitting.*

Manmohan What's the matter?

Balbir Why give it to me brother? Put a stamp on each note and mail it off in the morning. Make them happy. They'll go on singing your praises won't they? Maybe they'll build a statue.

Manmohan *can smell* **Balbir**'s *breath. He stoops down and grasps him by the back of the neck. He pulls his face close to his own.*

Manmohan Eh kee ah Balbir?

Balbir *pulls away and takes another swig from the bottle.*

Balbir My medicine brother. It makes me dream.

Manmohan *slaps him suddenly with the back of his hand then recoils, rubbing the offending hand.* **Balbir** *stands behind him.*

So you know the smell of it? And you a pukka Sikh! How do you know the smell? Did your daddy teach you?

Manmohan You're going mad Balbir.

Balbir The biggest, proudest Singh in the village, strutting around. Where did all that courage of his come from?

Manmohan *goes and turns on the light. A pause.*

Manmohan Now talk Balbir. Tell me about our father.

Balbir *turns back to the window.*

Tell me?

Balbir There's so much I could tell you. But your ears are too stupid to listen.

Manmohan Tell me, I'll listen to you. Even if it kills me I will.

Balbir *looks down at the mantle piece and sees the cup of soil he had placed there. He picks it up and walks towards* **Manmohan** *with it.*

Balbir The things you cherished. Look at this mud. What is it? It's mud. Special mud? No. Not special. Just dirt.

Manmohan Yes. That is all it ever was. But it put clothes on our backs and food in our mouths. But now tell me about our father Balbir.

Balbir You want me to kill your dreams for you? Why should I?

He spits into the cup.

Manmohan You have no shame Balbir.

Balbir Is it dirtier now, this mud, this dirt? No. It's the same.

He smiles serenely at **Manmohan**, *then suddenly swings around and throws the cup against a wall. The walls of the room fall back slowly, opening out like a flower. Very bright lights simultaneously come up, like a sun beating down without mercy. Beyond the walls an arid landscape – brushland – perhaps with the vague impression of a river showing in the distance. The* **Second Man** *sits holding his spear. Next to him the* **Third Man** *lies sleeping. The* **Second Man** *is stroking his sleeping companion's hair.* **Manmohan** *wanders out into the wilderness.* **Balbir** *stays at the periphery of what was the room.*

Second Man The Dravidians, the Aryans, the Pathans, the Persians, the Afghans, the Turks, the Jats. They've all fought their way into this place, crossed the six rivers and lain down in its cradle. Alexander and his Greeks marched on this soil and tasted its wonders and left their blood in its natives. A million years our bones and ashes have piled up to make mountains. Our gods here fought their wars and still fight. Our temples became ruins so we built new temples. It's a home for heroes. (*Pause.*) Look at him sleeping will you? He's an old man but now his dreams are like a child's. Like the first child of the first tribe from Africa that found this place and made it theirs.

Balbir You won't chain me down Manmohan. Not any more. I have a world in my skull, a plan, a map of creation. I have schemes, unholy desires.

Manmohan I can hear the water running under my feet. Come and listen. I can see the mountain ranges. Can you feel the wind against you? How it makes you stand like a man?

Second Man What must we be to be men? We must hate and kill and love our children. We must be warriors and priests.

Balbir *draws his 'kirpan' (sword).*

We'll cut one another to pieces. Because there must be blood in the soil to make it whole.

Balbir *slowly closes on* **Manmohan**. **Manmohan** *does not look at him, but draws his own kirpan.*

Manmohan Where do the stars go when the sky is blue? Where do the rivers run to?

The lights start to dim.

Balbir You're closing your eyes brother.

Manmohan I can feel my skin turning to a crust.

Balbir We'll live like corpses, you and me.

Manmohan I can feel the ground slipping away. Dead sand between my toes.

Balbir We'll laugh when they burn us.

Manmohan I can hear the raindrops drowning.

Balbir What did you expect then? Tell me, my brother.

Blackout.

Act Two

Scene 1

Dim lights go up on the platform, stage left. The sounds of heavy machinery – and the suggestion of great heat. **Manmohan** *enters carrying a crate which he stacks onto a pallet laid on the ground – he carries on doing this. The action in this scene should merge with that of the next scene towards its end – the boundaries between the two worlds becoming slightly blurred. After some time of stacking crates,* **Manmohan** *stops his work and walks slightly forward; he clasps his hands and kneels down as if to pray.*

Manmohan Vai Guru, vai guru.

He prays to himself in a silent whisper. As he does so another of the Indian workers enters and sits down to one side on a box watching him.

Worker Who is it for? (**Manmohan** *looks around.*) Do you think our God can hear us from here? Has he such excellent hearing?

Manmohan (*ending his prayer*) Vai guru jee ka Khalsa, vai guru jee ke futhe. (*He stands.*)

Worker No, I'm only joking. Yaar. His hearing must be second to no other Gods. It's tea break time. You want to go to the canteen?

Manmohan *shakes his head.*

Come on, it's good.

Manmohan *again shakes his head.*

We sit down and do chatting-fatting, that's all. People tell jokes. (*Pause.*) We're all friends. Come down, come on, yaar!

Pause. **Manmohan** *looks down at the ground.*

Well I can stay here to talk then. My

name's Jarnail, Jarnail Singh Chohal from Ludhiana. Pukka Punjabi. (*Short pause.*) What's your name?

Manmohan Manmohan Singh.

Worker Ever been to Ludhiana?

Manmohan Once only.

Worker It's a lovely town isn't it. It's a lovely place.

Manmohan Yes.

Worker Where are you from mister mystery man?

Manmohan A village.

Worker A village boy, eh?

Manmohan Bura Pind, near Jullunder.

Worker Yes, Bura Pind, I know Bura Pind, I passed through there once . . . On the bus . . . (*Pause.*) Are you a Khalsa, a holy man?

Manmohan I just have my own prayers. I never learned them.

Worker It doesn't matter too much the way a prayer is said. Long as you get it all in, eh? (**Manmohan** *goes off and fetches another crate.*) I do my best with them as well. They're a comfort sometimes aren't they. You got a wife waiting in Bura Pind?

Manmohan Yes.

Worker I knew there'd be someone, handsome lad like you. Is she a good girl? Look, it's break-time, yaar! There's going to be a meeting. We all have to go. (**Manmohan** *continues to fetch boxes.*) Sit down for a bit. How long can you carry on like this? Look . . . really . . . look . . . The men are starting to . . . Look . . . you keep so quiet and work double . . . they say . . . it's just . . . (*He grabs* **Manmohan** *by the arm.*) They think you're trying to basically arse-lick. It's not the way. They will just fuck us up. (*Pause.*) You should understand . . . We have learned some hard-hard lessons! They will cut us to small pieces and eat us up. (*Looking around. Then with a hushed tone.*) Our union! Our union says go to hell! They sell us out to the bosses without blinking an eyelid. They have a good giggle at our expense, the bastards! What does our God say to that, eh Guru? You can't turn your back on us. We only have each other. (*Pause. Then* **Manmohan** *pulls away and goes to fetch another box.*) Fine! I'll tell them what you say! You have it your way Mr Guru! But don't come crying to us when they squeeze your balls!

Worker *exits.* **Manmohan** *comes back onstage with another box, which he lays down on the ground – not on the stack he has been making. He looks at his hands, then, as the main stage is gradually illuminated, at what is going on in the room (i.e. the action of the next scene).*

Scene 2

The room, evening. We hear laughter, then **Balbir** *enters followed by* **Jane.** *He is carrying a bottle of vodka and smoking a cigarette. He goes and places the bottle on the table, then fetches two teacups.*

Balbir And this is my palace!

Jane (*looking around*) Well, Princes must have gone down in the world since they wrote all the stories.

Balbir (*he pours vodka into the cups. Taking the cigarette from his mouth*) This is nice.

Jane You haven't coughed yet.

Balbir (*pleased*) No! (*He takes a cup over to her.*)

Jane You're mean t' suck it right in then cough.

Balbir *takes a deep inhalation from the cigarette, walks over to the bed while holding his breath, then turns to her and blows out without coughing. He smiles at her.*

You got iron lungs?

Balbir Come here.

Jane (*smiling*) For what? (*He holds his hand out and she goes to him.*)

Balbir You smell pretty.

Jane Pretty what? You haven't told me your name.

Balbir *leans over and whispers something in her ear. She laughs. He starts to kiss her neck. Then he picks her up and lies her on the bed.*

You're wicked you are.

Balbir *stands and starts to strip off. The lights dim on the room and fade up on* **Manmohan** *still on platform stage left. He stands looking at his hands, then turns his gaze to* **Balbir** *and* **Jane** *as they start to make love.*

Manmohan I can still see where the rocks in the soil scratched my hands. I can see in the dark like a cat. Through the streets and houses. Through your shirt I can see even your heart pumping. What does a heart pump? What . . . and also why? Answer me those questions Balbir, like you used to answer everything in the fields.

The lights dim on **Manmohan.** *As they go back up on the room we hear the groans of* **Balbir** *and* **Jane** *copulating. There is a loud groan from* **Balbir.** **Jane** *strokes his head.*

Jane Good . . . good. (*Pause.*) Are you O.K.? (*He groans again.*) You got excited didn't you? (**Balbir** *rolls off her.*) It was nice though. (**Balbir** *laughs.*) It was. Don't you believe me?

Balbir Of course. How could I not believe?

Jane Good. I would't lie anyway.

Balbir Why?

Jane Sorry?

Balbir Why not lie?

Jane I just wouldn't.

Balbir Oh. 'Just wouldn't.' (*He gets up. Goes and gets a cigarette from his jacket and lights up.*) Tell me your name then.

Jane I told you already. (*Pause. He smiles at her.*) Elizabeth.

Balbir Elizabeth. Like the Queen.

Jane You knew that. Did you forget?

Balbir No. (*Going to her purse and opening it he empties out the contents and starts to go through it.*)

Jane Leave it. Those are my things! (*She jumps out of bed.* **Balbir** *is opening out a letter.*) Who d'you think you are, those are mine! (*She tries to grab the letter. It tears.* **Balbir** *gives it to her*) Look what you've done. I hate you!

Balbir Jane. It's a nice name.

Jane Don't talk to me you!

Balbir I'm sorry. (*Going over and touching her.*) Please. You're so beautiful Jane. I wanted to know.

Jane Why?

Balbir I'm just a stupid man. Your lips are so fresh. (*He kisses her.*) A little lie is nothing. It's like dust.

Jane No it isn't. We need lies to live. You had no right to do that did you? (*He kisses her again.*) I'm too soft I am. I'm no good at this. (*Pause. She starts to dress.*) I should go now.

Balbir Why?

Jane I have to make a living. (*Pause.*) Can I have the money please.

Balbir *goes back to the bed and sits down.*

You knew you'd have to.

Balbir Stay with me.

Jane I would. I like you.

Balbir Like me?

Jane Me mum used t' say I'm too quick to decide. But you can waste your whole life on decisions and still make the wrong ones. It's all first impressions with me. Don't you think that's the best way? I do. (*Pause.*) I saw you in the pub long before you saw me. I liked the way you moved. I knew you'd want me.

Balbir You knew this?

Jane I think I knew. I kind of made a wish. You know. Made a wish.

Pause.

Balbir You wished for the money in my pocket Jane.

Jane If you want one kind of life, a life that belongs to you, then you have to give away a part of yourself. I'm a martyr like Christ. (*She laughs.*) Will you give me the money?

Balbir Yes. How do you want to live?

Jane Why would you care? I don't know. Don't ask me. I don't want heaven. Well, I do. Everyone does. But I know that life I don't want. No money in my pocket. No faith in anyone. No chances. No true love. (*Gently mocking herself.*) True love.

Balbir I know the things you want. (*He goes over to her.*) In every detail.

Jane Do you?

Balbir *kisses his way down her body until he is kneeling before her. He kisses between her legs. She closes her eyes, quivering slightly.*

How could you know ?

She looks down at his head. She opens his hair and shakes it out.

Look at you. Like a girl.

Balbir (*standing up*) No Jane.

Jane Like a man? Why do you have it like that?

Balbir I am a Sikh. Our tenth Guru made us warriors.

Jane To fight us against what?

Balbir (*smiling*) The whole world.

Jane I don't believe that..

Balbir I want to fuck you again.

Jane (*after a pause*) Please don't talk to me like that.

He strokes her hair, then suddenly grabs it and drags her struggling to the bed. He falls on top of her.

No please don't. Balbir don't!

Balbir (*getting off her*) Fuck off then! (*He goes to his jacket and takes some notes. He throws them at her.*) Take it. (*He takes the rest of the money from his pockets.*) Take it all! Go on! Get out!

Jane I wasn't saying no. I was just . . . Come here. Come here. (*He goes to her.*) You don't know do you? You're clumsy, that's what. But I'll kiss you. Look. I'll kiss every part of you.

She kisses him. Then she stands up and starts to take off her clothes again. The lights go back up on **Manmohan**, *platform stage left, still in the factory.*

Manmohan You have to work. For money, to eat, to cover your naked body. You have to work, because God said toil hard and sow your crops and reap the fat of the land as your reward. You have to work alone. You have to swallow the pain. Balbir, hold me in your arms and tell me we must do all these things.

The lights dim on **Manmohan** *and go up on the room again.* **Balbir** *sits on the bed with* **Jane** *kneeling behind him. She is combing* **Balbir***'s hair.*

Jane Do you understand?

Balbir Of course I do.

Jane I hate being on the streets. Could you care about me . . . the way I am.

Balbir (*turning to her*) Tell me. How hard would you work? How hard, for us . . . for me.

Jane For you?

Balbir Yes.

Jane What about me, Balbir?

Balbir (*he holds her to himself*) I would join you to my flesh. Like the most sacred part of my soul.

Jane Men like me. Like when you saw me. They want me.

Balbir Oh, my Jane. Those brown boys, they'll be bursting at the seams. But all the time you'll be mine.

Jane If I did these things for you . . . How much would you do for me, Balbir?

Balbir Everything.

Jane What really? Tell me.

Balbir *looks at her, then fetches his kirpan. He unsheaths it.*

Balbir (*handing it to her*) You decide.

He sits down with his back to her.

Jane Shall I really? (*He does not reply. She starts to gently slice off his hair.*) It's beautiful. It's so beautiful. Have you ever cut it before?

Balbir No.

Jane Never in your whole life?

Balbir Never.

She hugs him. Blackout.

Scene 3

On the Platform, stage right. Lights up on the **Second** *and* **Third Men**. *The* **Second Man** *is crouching over the body of a traveller that he has just killed, the head on his spear is further decomposed.*

Third Man Is 'e dead?

Second Man Good as. Broke me blade on 'is spine. (*He starts to search the corpse's pockets.*) Nothing.

Third Man He seemed a pleasant sort. (*Looking at corpse's hands.*) Look, his life-line ends abruptly. Coat looks good.

Second Man (*taking the coat off the corpse*) Alright. Let's 'ave it off 'im then. For you.

Third Man Thanks, I needed one a lot. I get too cold. (*Pause.*) Ten miles 'e said. About ten.

Second Man He's on a longer trek now. I wonder which way he's heading. What secrets he's learned.

Third Man You wanna go in to the town?

Second Man Could be bad. We might get caught up in some serious shit.

Third Man I've had enough. (*He turns showing off the coat.*) What you reckon?

Second Man Bit small.

Third Man Small bloke.

Second Man Hole in the back.

Third Man Does it notice?

Second Man A bit. 'E bloody noticed it I'll tell ya, yelping like a dog.

Third Man I'll sew it.

Second Man I can feel the earth shiver.

Pause.

Third Man People maybe? People movin'? What's gonna happen?

Second Man We'll live and die. Then barefoot children will dance upon us and call us mud. They'll grow and stand on our shoulders and lick water from the clouds. Then they too will fall and join us. Come one.

Scene 4

Early morning. Saturday. Enter **Manmohan** *returning home from the night shift. He opens the door slowly, and enters very quietly. He sets down his lunch-box on the table, then goes over to the paraffin heater and warms himself by it. After a while he takes off his coat and scarf, hangs them up, then goes and sits down. He looks at the bed upon which* **Balbir** *is sleeping.*

After a few moments he goes to the window (which has the curtains drawn) and peeks out. He then takes a packet from his trouser pocket and opens it – it contains his wages. He holds the packet to his nose and – with eyes closed – takes a deep inward breath. Then he goes over to the table, and one by one lays out four or five notes upon it, after which he shakes a few coins out of the packet. These coins are then laid with care over the notes. **Manmohan** *also takes out a letter which he lays next to the other things.* **Balbir** *awakens and sits up in bed – his hair has been cropped.* **Jane** *is also in bed – but is shielded for the moment by* **Balbir. Manmohan** *stares at him.*

Balbir (*yawning*) You like my new hairstyle Manmohan? Modern style. Tony Curtis. Make me a cup of tea.

Pause. **Manmohan** *fingers the notes on the table. Then he gathers them up and goes to put them in the 'hiding place' they have made – for example under a loose floorboard.*

You should find a bank maybe. That is not a very safe place. (**Manmohan** *looks at him.*) Your money could be eaten by mice. Just think, eh. (*He smiles broadly.* **Manmohan** *gets up and goes to the window.*)

Make a cup of tea. (*Pause.*) A cup of tea for your brother. A cup of tea. A cup, a cup of tea. A cup of tea.

Manmohan *turns to look at him. They stare.*

A cup of tea.

Manmohan *does not move.* **Balbir** *gets up –*

naked – and pulling the blanket off the bed wraps it around himself. This leaves **Jane** *lying naked. She gives a squeal of surprise and attempts to shield herself with her hands.*

Balbir Oh, excuse me. Jane Manmohan, Manmohan Jane.

Balbir *faces him running his fingers through his hair.*

Does it bother you?

Pause.

Do you like it? Are you jealous?

Manmohan No Balbir. I pity you.

Balbir You pity me! Well that's good, I'm glad.

Jane Hello.

Balbir *smiles and walks out.* **Jane** *is attempting to hide herself from* **Manmohan** *– who does not look directly at her other than an occasional glimpse. He goes to his bed and fetches a blanket which he uses to cover* **Jane**.

Jane Thank you Manmo . . . ?

Manmohan Manmohan.

Jane He told me all about you. Are you angry? Don't get angry.

Manmohan Has he . . . are you . . .

Jane You won't know if you don't ask.

Manmohan Has he married you?

Jane Sorry?

Manmohan No. I know. You are very pretty.

Jane Am I?

Balbir *re-enters carrying one cup of tea.*

Balbir Oh what a gentleman! Did he get a good eyeful first eh?

Jane No, he didn't.

Balbir You want to be acquainted with Jane sometime? She is very good. Aren't you Jane? Jane knows all the secrets men harbour behind their eyes. Don't you Jane?

Jane I know enough I suppose.

Manmohan None of us know enough. Most of us know nothing.

Manmohan *goes and sits on his bed.* **Balbir** *goes to the table where he picks up the letter and starts to read.*

Balbir Look at my brother. He is a simple man.

Jane You just back from work Manmohan?

Manmohan Yes.

Jane Where d'you work?

Manmohan In . . .

Balbir In a factory. Same one I am quitting from tomorrow. (*He gives a broad smile.*) So your wife's family have got money to throw away. What does a woman want here? She will only be in the way. (**Manmohan** *ignores this.* **Balbir** *smiles.*) But I will do my best to make her feel welcome. She is my sister. I'll . . . respect her wishes.

Scene 5

Two months later. Lights go up on the empty room. We hear laughter then **Manmohan** *enters carrying suitcases. He is followed by* **Surinder**, *who has been joking with* **Balbir**.

Surinder When did you become a goonda like this? When did he do it?

Balbir Don't you like it? Tony Curtis – film star style.

Surinder Film star style? Your brother wants to be a film star Manmohan.

Manmohan He is handsome like a star.

Balbir Oh yes look at me. Handsome. (*Pause.*) Well sister?

Manmohan I will cook you something.

Balbir (*lightly*) That's her job now. Now we relax.

Surinder Listen to him, listen to lazy.

Balbir Lazy? Tell her Manmohan! Tell your wife!

Manmohan He works very hard.

Balbir I am therefore insulted!

Surinder Oh-ho! So this is not the exact same Balbir who used to sleep hiding behind a tree in the afternoons when everybody worked? This cannot be the Balbir who became a flying, invisible ghost during the harvest. That was some other Balbir?

Balbir Your wife is very mouthy. I will wack her bottom!

Manmohan What shall I cook?

Surinder Leave cooking Manmohan. Look at you! Oh it's so good to look at you again.

Balbir I've looked after him well sister, kept him safe. You been a good girl?

Manmohan Would you like to see the kitchen?

Surinder When are you moving out?

Balbir Pardon me?

Surinder (*to* **Manmohan**) Or ... (**Balbir** *exaggeratedly cleans out his ears with his fingers.*) ... When do we move?

Manmohan This is our room.

Surinder How can we live like this stupid, all three of us side by side?

Balbir She's right you know, no chance of funny business. Don't worry sister, I'll be discreet like a cockroach.

Manmohan Finding a place is not so easy Surinder.

Surinder Especially when you are not looking at all.

Balbir Oooh, snake's tongue. You picked yourself a sharp one Manmohan.

Manmohan I ... yes.

Balbir We'll be very cosy, very cosy.

Surinder *glares at* **Manmohan**.

Manmohan There is plenty of time to look. Something will come up.

Balbir (*going over to the bed*) You'll love the bed, you two. (*He bounces on it.*) It's a bloody fine bed ... I've thoroughly tested it you know.

Pause.

Manmohan Shall we unpack these?

Surinder I'm very tired.

Manmohan You want to sleep?

Balbir It's daytime. We can go for a walk.

Manmohan You want to look around?

Surinder I'm just tired.

Manmohan Yes, you should sleep.

Balbir Oh, look at this.

Manmohan What?

Balbir Such concern. So lovey-dovey already. So, how are things back home sister? Any news?

Surinder Plenty.

Balbir Plenty? Don't tell me ... big news ... don't tell me.

Surinder Alright.

Balbir Come on, what?

Surinder I'll tell Manmohan.

Balbir Go on, tell Manmohan.

Surinder Alone.

Balbir What?

Surinder Husband-wife talk.

Balbir Oh, husband-wife talk, eh? What's the big secret?

Manmohan (*making to exit*) You want a cup of tea? I'll do it milky.

Balbir I don't like this arrogance.

Surinder I'm married to him, not to you.

Balbir She's never liked me. (*To Manmohan.*) You know that.

Manmohan She does, she likes you.

Pause.

Balbir I can see how this is going to turn out.

Surinder You stopped sending money.

Manmohan I send from both of us.

Balbir No illusions please. You sent from yourself!

Surinder You stopped writing. Not even a word on Manmohan's letters. Nothing. Zero.

Balbir I had no news to convey. We lead a boring life. I am not fond of sentimental repetition. (*Pause.*) What exactly are you getting at? I want the heart of the matter. You're a clever girl so place your finger on it for me.

Surinder Loyalty.

Balbir Yes?

Surinder That's what they're saying back home.

Manmohan That's not fair Surinder.

Surinder No?

Balbir Loyalty!

Manmohan Things have been . . .

Surinder Don't spit on the word . . .

Manmohan They . . .

Balbir (*angrily*) Loyalty!

Manmohan They . . . (*He gives up.*)

Surinder You want me to lend you a dictionary?

Balbir (*making to go out*) You've got a woman there Manmohan. She's got mouth muscles and that's a fact. (*He leaves then comes back.*) Ten seconds flat since her feet kissed the ground, ages since she's seen either of us, and she starts up like this!

Surinder You asked me!

Balbir (*leaving*) Pah!

Surinder *sits down on the bed.*

Surinder I want to go home.

Manmohan Yes.

Pause.

Surinder Do you want me here?

Manmohan Yes.

Pause.

Surinder Have you slept with other women? (*Pause.*) Don't tell me if you don't want to.

Manmohan No, I never.

Surinder Never wanted to?

Pause.

Manmohan I have wanted to.

Surinder Many times?

Manmohan Some times.

Surinder Good, you're normal then! I've got my B.A. you know and I'm cleverer than you.

Manmohan The first is a great achievement. The second is not uncommon I'm afraid.

Surinder I'll get a job. I'll pull my weight. Don't think I won't. I'll pull my weight plus a bit.

Manmohan Your eyes are darker now. They used to be light brown. (*She holds out her hands to him.*) And your hands. They're still strong. Beautiful fingers. (*He kisses her hands.*)

Surinder I don't want to kiss you yet Manmohan. Do you mind? (**Manmohan** *looks puzzled.*) We're almost strangers now. I need . . . before . . .

Short pause.

Manmohan I'll make tea then.

Surinder Yes. (*He exits. She looks round and begins to unpack.*) I've got presents . . . for both of you.

Scene 6

Platform, stage right. It is night-time. **Balbir** *and* **Jane** *stand beneath a street lamp in Shepherds Bush.*

Balbir You were late.

Jane Sorry.

Balbir Three hours.

Jane You should've gone home. I'm sorry.

Balbir Why?

Jane What?

Balbir Three hours? I looked everywhere like a hungry dog.

Jane There was no need for you to wait. It was my own time.

Balbir (*pulling her back by the hair*) Nothing is yours. Nothing.

Jane Stop it.

Balbir Oh god! Why don't you understand? You gave yourself to me.

Jane Not like this! Not my whole life.

Balbir Your body is mine, your blood is mine, your sweat and tears mine, your shit and piss mine.

She tries to pull herself away. He slaps her hard across the face then forces her to look into his eyes.

Balbir The only men you will have are the men I give you. No other fuckers. You sold your sweet soul my darling.

Jane (*trying to push him away*) Bastard! You don't own any part of me!

Balbir No? No? (*Grabbing between her legs.*) This I own! (**Jane** *is silenced.*) This I own. This thing that I bought.

Jane (*starting to sob*) You're hurting me.

Balbir Look what you have made of me Jane. What kind of man have you constructed?

Jane I haven't done nothing to you. Don't blame me for what you are Balbir.

Balbir This thing is warm. How many pounds and pence did your passion divine? Did you think you might turn away? Would you turn away from me? Would you burn in hell alone?

Jane Please.

He tightens his grip, increasing the pain.

I'm sorry. I'm sorry.

Balbir *kisses her.*

Scene 7

The rubber factory. Lights go up on the platform, stage left. **Manmohan** *is cleaning up with a broom. A* **White Worker** *enters, carrying a newspaper. He sits on a crate watching* **Manmohan**.

White Worker Eh, let me tell you something.

Manmohan *stops stacking.*

I can look at a man you know, an' tell things. Wha'ss your star sign?

Pause. **Manmohan** *does not reply.*

Why did you come. Tell me about it. Why did you come? (*Pause.* **Manmohan** *starts working again.*) You're not a conversationalist exactly are you? Given that I'm a man expressing a genuine interest without pisstake. Given that you are a man who, if appearances and whispers are anything to go by, could do with a friend.

Pause. **Manmohan** *stops.*

Manmohan This is not my job.

White Worker Yeah?

Manmohan You took me off my job.

White Worker Yeah. I did. Can't deny it.

Manmohan And make me do this.

White Worker You don't like it? You can leave it.

Manmohan How many nights will I have to . . .

White Worker Many as I say. Put in a complaint if you want. Unfair treatment. Union should do something. (*Pause.*) I'm the convenor, so you can lodge a complaint right now if you wanna.

Manmohan *continues to work.*

None of your bunch like me. They say I got no father.

White Worker *spits on the floor in front of* **Manmohan**.

Ohh, what a mess.

Pause. **Manmohan** *stares at him.*

You got an air about you I don't like. It's your job to wipe that up. Go on, do your job.

Pause. **White Worker** *stands.*

You're a proud man I think. Pride. Oh that's something. Pride dies a death in these surroundings. Wipe it up.

Pause. **Manmohan** *takes a rag from his pocket and wipes up the spit.* **White Worker** *smiles.*

You must be desperate boy. (*Pause. Then he spits again on the floor.*)

Ooh. Another one. Go on. (**Manmohan** *does not move.*) Go on. Don't mind me!

Manmohan *throws down the rag.* **White Worker** *smiles, picks it up and puts it in* **Manmohan**'s *hand. He then puts his other hand on his shoulder and tries to force* **Manmohan** *down to the floor.*

You need some help?

However, he finds that he cannot move **Manmohan**. **Manmohan** *takes a hold of one of* **White Worker**'s *fore-arms and slowly pushes him away. He then tightens his grip on* **White Worker**'s *arm, gradually forcing him to the ground. They freeze,* **White Worker** *looking up at* **Manmohan** *with a look of near terror.*

Manmohan Pride. Pride. Pride.

Scene 8

Balbir *is lying on his bed reading.* **Surinder** *comes in and out of the room making herself busy with washing and tidying. She brings in some clothes that she has washed and puts them on an airer. She then takes the alarm clock and a screwdriver – sits at a table – and starts to open up the back of the clock.*

Balbir These evenings will be long and lonely for you.

Surinder He has to work just like all of us . . . Like some of us.

Balbir Oh, I pay my way, sister. And you. Are you enjoying the job my brother begged them to give you?

Surinder It's work and money to me, that's all. 'Enjoying' does not come into it. We will save and buy our house. That's all I want.

Balbir The factory is not good for a woman. You will become lonely and then bitter.

Surinder Or I might just get used to it.

Balbir Maybe you will. But then what kind of woman will you be? (*Pause.*) What are you doing?

Surinder The alarm's stopped working.

Balbir So you want to mess it up even more? (**Surinder** *looks up.*) Oh no, of course you won't sister.

A knock on the door, enter **Landlord**.

Landlord Ah-ha!

Balbir Hello.

Landlord So! You slimy character!

Balbir How are you and the lady wife?

Landlord Vos dreaming I asked myself? I see voman go in an' out, I hear voman's voice all times day an' night. I remember agreement we make – but I reasonable man – I say to wife, this is temporary situation, we give them time to remedy. But my good wife's patience is at end of tether my friend!

Balbir Yes, this is my beloved sister-in-law. She has to come to live.

Landlord I vish not to utter profanities in mixed company, but I specified with you only two.

Balbir (*getting up*) There was no written agreement.

Landlord I make crystal clear.

Balbir So?

Landlord So? So? You break word and say 'so'?

Balbir What do you want?

Landlord The restoration of honour.

Pause. Smiling **Balbir** *takes a roll of notes from his pocket. He unpeels the notes slowly.*

Balbir Honour. Yes I appreciate honour.

He lays the notes in his hand.

Landlord In future, no compromize.

Balbir *counts out some more notes.*

Balbir Now, fuck off eh?

He smiles, the **Landlord** *glares.*

Landlord The Lord is my witness!

He exits. Pause.

Surinder Can you take that bloody Jesus picture off the wall?

Balbir (*looking at it above his bed*) I quite like it. He has watched over me.

Surinder Well I'll watch over you now.

Balbir (*getting up and taking down the picture and crucifix*) Will you sister? (*He goes over to the table.*) Well that's nice. (*He puts the items down.*) Do I disturb you?

Surinder Disturb? No.

Balbir I mean, emotional disturbance. A quiver of the bones.

Surinder My bones are very well.

Balbir Yes?

Surinder Yes.

Balbir Sure?

Surinder Sure.

Balbir I've seen you looking at me.

Surinder You don't want me to look when you talk?

Balbir Those hungry eyes biting into me. Chewing on me.

Surinder Do I give you nightmares?

Balbir You give me all kinds of dreams. (*He starts to caress her shoulders, then moves his hands towards her breasts.*)

Surinder I'm your brother's wife Balbir.

Balbir 'My brother's wife'. Is that a brand of chastity belt?

Surinder (*she stands suddenly and turns*) Haramzada!

Balbir Call me anything under the sun.

Go on. I love your hate of me. (*He grabs her.*) All my thoughts are of love and death. (*He kisses her mouth. She pulls away.*)

Surinder What kind of animal are you?

Balbir The kind that slips through blades of grass.

Surinder Yes.

Balbir I have no illusions. I can't have your soul, perhaps not, but I can have . . .

Surinder Manmohan would kill you.

Balbir I'm already dead. (*He kisses her. Pause.*) You know my story Surinder.

Surinder I know it. But now God will damn you.

Balbir I'll laugh when he does.

Surinder It will happen Balbir. In the village they would drag you screaming through the fields for this. They would shit on your dirty face.

Balbir Yes.

Surinder And I would be one of them.

Balbir I don't want forgiveness then. Here . . . my actions have no . . .

Surinder Balbir, please Balbir.

Balbir They have no . . .

Surinder Balbir.

Balbir . . . Consequences.

Pause. She relaxes slightly, then leans forward and kisses him. They go into a passionate embrace. They fall onto the bed. **Balbir** *starts to pull off* **Surinder**'s *clothes.* **Manmohan** *half-enters the room. He sees what is happening and watches. He seems about to say something.*

Surinder Balbir, I want you Balbir . . .

Manmohan *exits quietly.*

Scene 9

On the Platform, stage right. The **Second** *and* **Third Men** *stand looking out into the darkness. The head on the* **Second Man**'s *spear is now no more than a skull. The* **Third Man** *still carries the dead baby.*

Third Man These winds 'r' getting sharper. (*He puts a finger into his mouth.*) I can feel it in me teeth.

Second Man We should be poets.

Third Man You reckon?

Second Man To describe what we've seen. This abundant wasteland. The lives lost. These God-forsaken times.

Third Man This coat. It's the best I've had. 'Cept for the hole which I'll fix someday.

Second Man I thought you came out of money. What d'you know of fixing.

Third Man I was idle in my youth. That's true. What is this place?

Second Man Are there places anymore? We cannot say. They'll burn the old maps.

Third Man There was a bloke back there. Far off, but I could just see. I shouted. You were a world away. He looked as if he was heading places.

Second Man He'll be lost too soon.

Third Man Lost? (*Grabbing him.*) Don't fuck about. I'm spooked up. Where are we?

Second Man Let's build a fire. Let's cook small animals and leftovers and sing songs. What do you say? Let's have us a good time!

Third Man No, no, no. Don't string me along.

Second Man We're here. You strang along. (*He touches his face.*) Wait with me now. Loosen your clothes and tell me your most secret dreams.

Third Man I'm hungry. We've got no small animals or leftovers. We drink our own piss for thirst. I've had it. I wanna go back.

Second Man Sit with me. Come on. We'll point our toes down, cross these legs and fingers of ours, blow our noses . . .

Third Man No, I don't know why. I'm lonely, I have a constant yearnin' for the way things were.

Second Man . . . And we'll wait.

Scene 10

Two weeks later. **Manmohan** *is asleep in his bed. Enter* **Jane**, *closely followed by* **Balbir**. *She is obviously upset, and puts as much distance between herself and* **Balbir** *as possible.* **Balbir** *stares at her, then paces about trying to put his thoughts in order.*

Balbir (*suddenly throwing up his arms*) My darling! (*He moves towards her.*)

Jane (*almost shouting*) Don't, don't, don't!

Balbir (*gesturing to* **Manmohan**) Shhh!

Jane You won't let me think. I . . .

Balbir No. Don't speak. Just listen. There are things I must say. (*Sitting on a chair.*) I have curious dreams. (*Pause.*) I take long walks and bus rides. All around London. I like walking in dark little places where few people go. I peer into comfortable houses and through the skulls of stupidly contented people that live and die in the manner of insects. The mothers suckle their children with poisoned breasts and whisper filthy lies into their ears. I see and know this. It makes me sick. Yet I pity them for their . . . insignificance. (*Pause.*) This city has fixed itself in my brain, it burns my head. (*Pause.*) I want its secret. This strange secret that drew us like moths.

(*Pause.*) Why are we attracted? (*Pause.*) You are a moth like me, Jane.

Jane No, we're different species altogether.

Balbir Perhaps.

Jane (*looking at* **Manmohan**) Even he's nothing like you. You're all by yourself.

Balbir How do you know what he's like?

Jane There's nothing more to talk over now. (*She makes to leave –* **Balbir** *stands up.*)

Balbir I thought you loved me.

Pause.

Then why are you denying yourself?

Jane You . . .

Balbir I would tear open my chest for you, if it would be a proof of my feelings. I cannot let you go.

Jane Oh Balbir don't.

Balbir (*closing in on her*) From the first moment I smelt your breath and felt your skin. Your sweet skin.

Jane No.

Balbir I have this passion . . . such a passion that my eyes are burning.

Jane You're eating me up! Leave me alone!

Balbir You can't leave me.

Jane We've never been together.

Balbir Now . . . be with me. Marry me!

Jane You wanted a whore to line your pockets. Now you're scared you'll have to work for it again.

Balbir Haven't I worked for you?

Jane Getting your mates to screw a white girl? Oh, that must have been so hard!

Balbir I kept you away from the streets. Out of the sewer!

Jane (*shouting*) Only to shove me in another one!

By this time **Manmohan** *has woken. He sits up in bed.*

I'm going far away Balbir.

Balbir Which white boy is whispering in your ear? Whose cock are you holding onto?

Jane I'm never coming back. That's it.

Balbir Where are you running to, Jane?

Jane I don't know. Birmingham.

Balbir Birmingham, really. Birmingham. I don't believe you.

Jane That doesn't matter now.

Balbir You don't have enough muscles to carry yourself that far. Who's the bastard? Who's the cock?

Jane Get out of my way.

Balbir (*smiling*) How many times has your father fucked you? How many times did you suck his cock for pocket money?

Jane is stunned. Then she attacks him screaming.

Jane No . . . no . . . no . . . (*With sudden anger.*) I hate you! You bastard! I'll kill you!

Manmohan *leaps out of bed and pulls them apart. He had to hold onto* **Jane** *who is becoming hysterical.*

Balbir Tell me his name you bitch. I'll tear out his throat.

Manmohan Leave her alone now!

Balbir She's made me crawl around in her shit. Look at her laughing at me.

Manmohan She's not laughing, she's crying.

Balbir *pulls out a knife and stabs* **Jane** *several times while* **Manmohan** – *who is stunned* – *still holds her.* **Manmohan** *drops* **Jane** *and struggles with* **Balbir** *for the knife.*

They eventually stand face to face, the knife – held aloft by both of them – pointing upwards. **Balbir** *stares into* **Manmohan**'s *eyes, then smiles and kisses him full on the lips. After a moment* **Manmohan** *pulls away in a daze. He walks slowly backwards and sits down on his bed.* **Balbir** *watches him – still smiling – then looks down at* **Jane** *who is dying.*

Balbir There's a mess for us to clean my brother.

Manmohan *buries his face in his hands and starts to sob.*

He puts the knife to his mouth and, looking intently at **Manmohan** – *almost victoriously* – *licks the blood from it. The lights fade on this, with only the sound of* **Jane**'s *dying grunts/pants and* **Manmohan** *sobbing to himself.*

Blackout.

Scene 11

Two spotlights go up. One on the door to the room, the other on **Manmohan** *sitting on his bed –* **Surinder** *asleep by his side. He is holding a pair of scissors and his hair is open. He begins to cut away his hair. Simultaneously,* **Balbir** *enters and goes to the place where the money is kept. He is wearing a large coat – his packed cases are by his bed. He takes all the money in the hiding place, picks up his bags and quietly leaves the room. The lights gradually dim on* **Manmohan** *ceremoniously cutting his hair.*

Act Three

Scene 1

As the lights go up the **Second** *and* **Third Men**, *still on the Platform stage right, are changing from their 1947 clothes into modern dress to become the* **Henchmen**.

The last few bars of the Indian National anthem echo as if played in a vast arena. Cheering crowds. The lights go up on Platform centre. Sounds of polite conversation. The **Indian Prime Minister**, *flanked by two* **Officials**, *greets* **Balbir**. *They are both holding glasses of whiskey.*

Balbir This is a grand honour for me sir.

Indian Prime Minister Mr . . .?

Balbir Balbir Singh, British Indian Businessmen's Federation, President elect.

Indian Prime Minister Of course, our rising star.

Balbir Sometimes it is difficult at my age to distinguish rising from setting.

Indian Prime Minister (*laughing politely*) I have had many glowing reports about your unrelenting labours on behalf of the Party . . . I am given to understand that you are one of our most skilled power-brokers on this side of the water.

Balbir Sir, power-blind and without purposeful end is something I despise utterly. No sir, I am betrothed to a higher goal. That is my raison d'être. The Nation occupies my soul sir. Yet Party and Nation are synonymous in my eyes. You are India!

Indian Prime Minister (*slightly embarrassed*) Er, you are too kind.

Balbir My loyalty, sir, is not something that I can conceal.

Indian Prime Minister I am sure you will not let the side down.

Balbir Unthinkable . . . My hair is cut, yet I am a devout pukka Sikh nonetheless. But in my mind the idea of being a true Sikh and a true Indian are inextricably linked. Will you be visiting the provinces . . . the soggy English countryside perhaps?

Indian Prime Minister Glenneagles. For the Summit.

Balbir Of course! . . . Do you mind . . . I mean . . . may I, for a moment . . .

Indian Prime Minister Surely. (*He gestures to his* **Officials** *and moves to one side with* **Balbir**.)

Balbir I know a man in your eminent position . . . You have no greater admirer.

Indian Prime Minister Thank you.

Balbir No, no, no thanks are needed. In fact the reverse, quite the contrary.

Pause.

Indian Prime Minister Is there some matter you wish to draw to my attention?

Balbir You see those two young ladies?

Indian Prime Minister Er, yes, I do.

Balbir They too are passionate admirers of your good self, as well as employees of mine. An arrangement could quite discreetly be made . . .

Indian Prime Minister (*almost licking his lips*) Mr Singh, you surprise me.

Balbir I consider myself a servant to the Nation, and thus to you. Those ladies are in essence artists. Men are their canvas. It would be an achievement for them to eternally cherish. There would be no question of indiscretion – I stake my own reputation on this. (*He takes out some photographs.*) Perhaps these might serve to illustrate my point.

Indian Prime Minister (*he takes the photos, his eyes widen and his mouth drops open*)

Yes . . . yes. Quite fascinating.

Balbir They are so wonderfully athletic. There should be an Olympic event especially designated – these two would win India the gold medal without a doubt.

Indian Prime Minister (*still looking at the pictures*) Yes, yes, indeed. Indeed.

Balbir I can personally vouch for that . . . We are men of the World, Sir, certain inevitable thirsts must be quenched.

Indian Prime Minister (*putting the photographs into an inside pocket*) If you speak to Sunil over there, he is my personal assistant. I am sure he will be able to make room in this evening's schedule.

Balbir I will tell them. They will be so excited, like ripe and giggling schoolgirls!

They both smile broadly.

Scene 2

Dim lights go up on the main playing area. It is the living room of **Manmohan**'s *house – 1987 – in Southall. The decor reflects a modest income.* **Manmohan** *sits watching an Indian video on his television set. After a few moments his son,* **Harjeet** *enters. He is a young athletic looking man of about twenty seven years of age. He is very smartly dressed in a dark suit.*

Harjeet Dad. (*Pause.*) I thought I'd be off now. I saw mum before she went this morning. We said our goodbyes. Tears all round you know. (*Pause.*) Don't mind me saying this dad. There's no contentment in her. I think she feels lost. (*Pause.*) I know it's something that you have to determine between you. She just needs some sign from you. I know you'll do that dad. You can take that step. I won't push it. I'm sorry. It's just

my reading. Who am I to know the affairs of your hearts. I can only guess. (*Pause.*) I went for a walk around. Thought I'd take in the atmosphere. The place is getting to be really up 'n' coming isn't it? A genuine boom town. It's strange how places change I think. But it seems to be a good thing, this process.

Manmohan For some, yes.

Pause.

Harjeet The men of power and wealth have taken history and geography into their hands it seems. You look at them. Country bumpkins when they were kids now sitting in big fat cars talking sub-O level English and rural Punjabi into their car phones. I am to some extent in awe of them.

Manmohan *nods. Pause.*

Still watching this stuff, are you? You want the sound up? (*Pause.*) Shall I turn if off? Which one is it? They all seem the same to me. (*Looking into the screen.*) I think I know that guy though. Maybe we should talk dad. (*Pause.*) She doing overtime tonight?

Manmohan Yes.

Pause.

Harjeet Yes . . . she mentioned it. Well, she has to now.

Manmohan We don't need the money anymore. There is nothing to do with the money.

Harjeet You know how it is with mum. She wants to go back, build a house and new life.

Manmohan We have had our life.

Harjeet She has romantic notions. I know. But they aren't impossible fantasies. You must give her desires some credence.

Manmohan I will die here.

Harjeet Don't talk like that dad. (*Going to the T.V.*) Look let me turn this off.

Manmohan Leave it!

Harjeet Shall I turn the sound up then?

Manmohan No. I know the story already. (*Pause* **Harjeet** *goes and sits down.*) You have become a big strong man Harjeet.

Harjeet Yep, just like my dad people say.

Manmohan Yes, just like your daddy.

Pause. **Manmohan** *gets up and turns off the TV.*

Harjeet Dad. You don't mind if I say something?

Manmohan Say anything, Harjeet.

Harjeet You have to pull yourself up out of it. There are other jobs. I mean O.K you did that same one for what . . . twenty odd years . . .

Manmohan Twenty eight years. Since before you were born.

Harjeet But it never got you anywhere. There was never a sense of progression. It was one long road without deviation. Please. There are other jobs. I'll check around. I don't really have to be back in Edinburgh for another day or so. The firm can wait.

Manmohan I am proud of you. A lawyer is an important man in our country. Don't worry for me, look to a bright life, a future.

Harjeet I can't leave you behind. I owe it to you and mum.

Manmohan No, we are in the past. Edinburgh is your future.

Harjeet I'm just saying to you that you can pull up out of this . . . this state of mourning you seem to be in. This attitude is pulling you away from the life you should be getting on with. I don't like to see it dad, I don't like to see it.

Manmohan Harjeet . . . the roof over our heads, the food in our mouths, the shoes on our feet – I worked for these valuable things.

Harjeet And got t' be a stranger to us. Mum pleaded for you to go on days.

Manmohan Yes.

Pause.

Harjeet I won't take it away from you dad, no way, I am not denigrating what you did. (*Pause.*) You know, when I see kids swanning around this town in the Gaultier suits their fathers put on their naked backs, I think how much money sits behind them. What confidence it must bestow! I really wonder about the awesome talent those men have got for bringing pound notes together in one place. I want to absorb that much from them. I want that talent.

Manmohan It is not magic they do. Some of them work hard, others lie and cheat, others never had to work for what they have.

Harjeet Suppose so. Funny though, around here, people like them living almost side by side with people like . . .

Manmohan People like us?

Harjeet Not the best kind of set up. Must make them nervy sometimes. I would move.

Pause.

This will sound stupid dad. (**Manmohan** *looks at him.*) What do you reckon on morality. How do you determine . . . how do you decide on these things?

Manmohan You do the right thing.

Harjeet And what is that?

Manmohan What is good.

Harjeet Yes, good, but for who?

Manmohan For your family. For your

village. For those you love.

Pause.

Harjeet (*quietly, almost to himself*) Yes.

Pause.

Manmohan I cook now.

Harjeet Good, that's good.

Manmohan I clean up.

Harjeet Looks good. The house looks good. (*Pause.*) You want your legs rubbed a bit? (**Manmohan** *smiles. Shakes his head.*) What are you thinking about?

Manmohan The same things. All the time.

Harjeet Penny for 'em?

Manmohan Penny?

Harjeet Your thoughts.

Manmohan I've been thinking. (*Pause.*) My life. (*Pause.*) About . . .

Pause. **Manmohan** *seems about to cry.*

Harjeet I've got ten K dad, ten thousand pounds. (*Pause.*) It's my money for this purpose. (*Pause.*) I'm going to hand it over to mum. For the India thing. That'll do it dad. You can go back.

Manmohan (*crying*) . . . My life.

Harjeet (*going to him*) No dad.

Manmohan So many stupid things. Oh my God.

Harjeet Please dad.

Manmohan (*grabbing* **Harjeet**) So many evil things! Such evils things! Don't ask me what is good, don't ask me that!

Harjeet What evil things dad?

Manmohan The things I did! The things I did!

Harjeet You've done nothing. What've you done?

Manmohan Why did I come here? Why did I come here? Why did I come here?

Harjeet You can go back.

Manmohan To what? Oh my God.

Harjeet Start over. Make a life there, you and mum.

Manmohan I was so weak.

Harjeet You did your best. You gave it a swing. A good swing.

Manmohan Why, why, why? Why (*Sobbing.*) Why?

Harjeet (*holding him*) I don't know dad.

Manmohan Nobody knows.

Harjeet You must know. You must have had a reason. All those years ago you had a reason.

Manmohan No.

Harjeet You must have.

Manmohan Your father was such a man. Such a man I . . .

Harjeet Don't talk about yourself as if you're dead.

Manmohan Life passes so quickly. When I was young I thought . . . I thought there was so much time.

Harjeet You've still got time.

Manmohan No, no more time now. No more time.

Harjeet It's for me to do now, to make our name in the world. It's time for both of you to rest. I know what people say. They look at what we've got, some of them sneer. But I'm going to turn everything around dad. I don't care what I have to do. Don't let that shock you. I was born on this island I know its secrets better than you ever could. I won't let time run me down. I swear to you dad, all over England they'll know me. And you'll be a part of that. I promise you.

The lights go down on the section of the room occupied by **Harjeet**. *Suddenly, the TV is illuminated with the image of* **Balbir**'s *face, aged about fifty, looking straight out at* **Manmohan**. **Manmohan** *does not respond in any way.*

Balbir's TV Image I've got the fear of God in me – Manmohan. I have every species of fear – Manmohan. I have collected them and stored them away – Manmohan. Young men grow old – Manmohan.

The screen image fades, together with the lights. **Manmohan** *still has not moved.*

Scene 3

On the platform – lights go up on a heated argument. **Balbir**, *now a man of about fifty years old is dressed in an expensive suit; the years have been kind to him. He is seated behind a large antique desk in his office which is situated in the centre of Edinburgh. On the wall is a large picture of* **Balbir** *standing next to a local white VIP, with a triumphant smile on his face (perhaps doing a large 'thumbs up' to the camera). His interlocutor is* **Harjeet**. *The action of this scene occurs one week after that of Scene One.*

Harjeet But I thought . . .

Balbir What – exactly?

Harjeet If you'd let me finish.

Balbir Finish!

Harjeet I thought it was quite clear. I was given the prerogative.

Balbir I put you in my trust! But I did not for a moment confer absolute autonomy.

Harjeet It was my jurisdiction. I had to determine the appropriate action.

Balbir Without consultation?

Harjeet At that time it didn't appear necessary.

Balbir Because your eyes were closed!

Harjeet Given the circumstances I think I acted correctly, given my place in the line of command. If I had anticipated your reaction.

Balbir It is your role, your function, to anticipate. You failed in that.

Harjeet Yes. We live and learn they say.

Balbir Who say?

Harjeet The wise men.

Balbir How many wise men you meet in the Edinburgh low-life? I was not aware of their existence in our midst. (*Pause.*) Do you know why you did this? Why you burned down the family home of one of our biggest customers?

Harjeet He was skimming, capitalizing on our implicit trust – we were losing revenue.

Balbir . . . And broke a variety of limbs amongst others.

Harjeet They were all active participants. I have reliable evidence. Independent corroboration.

Balbir The only reason I can discern is that you have no sense of what is proper, of precedent, of History.

Harjeet History?

Balbir My history. The history of this business.

Harjeet Of what relevance . . .

Balbir When I laid the foundations of this great edifice that you see now, I had to do many things which would, today, make me shudder. Those were brutal times. But always I knew that things would evolve. Integrity and honour have replaced brutality. We have established order in our realm. We have earned a certain . . . legitimacy. If years ago I had not thought this was possible . . . well, perhaps I would have packed my bags and gone back home. You are well educated, a degree in Law. I am surprised.

Harjeet History was never my subject. In any case, I was always uncomfortable studying something that I had no intention of adhering to. That's the problem with our legal system – it defies rational belief.

Balbir (*flapping his arms like wings, he rises out of his chair*) Behold and learn Harjeet. I am the phoenix, I have risen out of my burning ashes.

Harjeet That's a poetic thought. Does it have any tangible reference?

Balbir I find it difficult to be angry with you, Harjeet.

Harjeet I'm glad.

Balbir I can fully appreciate the pleasure you must have drawn from your actions. The heat of a raging fire. The screams of those poor middle-aged men as their bones were broken – the only anaesthetic being a kick in the kidneys.

Harjeet I assure you it was an objective decision. There were only financial considerations.

Balbir You can open your heart to me.

Harjeet My heart is not for the plucking, sir.

Balbir (*going round and putting his arm around* **Harjeet***'s shoulder*) I've taken you under my wing. You are like a son to me. Even though your father denies my very existence now, disowns me. I have treated you like my blood. You are my own blood!

Harjeet I don't intend to capitalize on whatever bond you may feel.

Balbir If it were not for that 'bond',

you would at this moment be in a casualty ward recovering – if you were fortunate – from your extensive injuries. On your inevitable return to the fold, you would be relegated to a minor role. As it is, you are escaping with a slap on the wrists. You must appreciate that in the side of the business you are working in, it is vital not to take action which might conceivably attract the attention of the Authorities. The government in its irrefutable wisdom has launched all these damn expensive advertizing campaigns. The big H is being equated with hellfire. That is bad publicity. You will not be regarded by the Courts as the social functionary which you in fact are. Even the Conservatives do not understand the true nature of the market – of genuine laissez faire. They still entertain these baseless moral platitudes.

Harjeet I should have been more subtle. Yes. I definitely can see your point.

Balbir There is a gradual intensity of pressure that you have at your disposal. Apply it sparingly. Ultimately these bastards that we do business with will rely upon us for their primary supplies. This is a monopoly situation. We have our region. Our security rests with our ability to effectively control this region. We cannot afford to tarnish our reputations with the unnecessary introduction of an iron fist.

Harjeet Well . . . I feel duly chastised and punished.

Pause. **Balbir** *turns and looks out of his office window.*

Balbir I can stand for hours and watch people and cars . . . all the little journeys that we compose our lives with.

Harjeet It's a good location.

Balbir I have made important friends. If one can call co-conspirators 'friend'.

Harjeet It's an immense achievement.

Balbir You know our P.M. wants me to act in an advisory capacity on certain matters.

Harjeet (*very surprised*) She's asked you to . . . Thatcher asked you to!

Balbir No, not Margaret. Our P.M. A fine upstanding young man.

Harjeet Well that's fantastic! When I step in here, well it's like entering a temple. I am genuinely in awe of you.

Balbir I've done a lot of work for Congress in our Community. Especially through the recent troubles. I even swung the Indian Businessmen's Federation behind the party line – those fat old buggers, political jellyfish to a man – do you know what that means for us in terms of diplomatic P.R?

Harjeet This was on the Khalistan thing?

Balbir Yes.

Harjeet It's getting serious.

Balbir The P.M. will deal with it. He has the political will and foresight.

Harjeet I mean here.

Balbir Yes.

Harjeet Certain individuals are taking out lucrative contracts. Certain fringe groups are equipping themselves for a small scale war. The word is that global blood revenge is going to be exacted for the actions taken against the temple in Amritsar.

Balbir When I look out over this city, I can sense the menace.

Harjeet We have to talk protection.

Balbir Of what?

Harjeet You'll be a prime target sir. It's a probability that they'll have a go.

Balbir Yes. They will want my blood.

Harjeet Effective defence against this type of thread – against terrorists – is very problematic. I think it's something I should be assigned to.

Pause.

Balbir Harjeet, if it were not too late already, I would tell you to lead a simple life.

Pause.

Harjeet I'll bear it in mind anyway. Am I on the case?

Balbir No. The echoes of our deeds resonate within us. The world senses that vibrance, and history closes around us. We are clenched in fists that will not tire.

Harjeet I can see that Uncle.

Balbir Can you? I am surprised.

Harjeet But it's of dubious pertinence to the matter at hand.

Balbir That may be.

Harjeet Who then? The men should be alerted. You should go underground until the threat is clearly identified.

Balbir It's too late.

Harjeet I don't understand. Is this some subtle deathwise you have? All it takes is a bomb strapped to an axle, or a singleminded and well-paid man with a gun. There is nothing metaphysical about the art of killing. It is something we can apprehend and deal with on a day to day level.

They are interrupted by the entrance of one of **Balbir**'*s employees – clearly some kind of general bodyguard, in his late thirties.*

Balbir I'm busy.

Bodyguard I know boss. I'm very sorry boss.

Balbir Well?

Bodyguard For your personal attention sir. An urgent matter.

Balbir Go on. (*The* **Bodyguard** *looks at* **Harjeet**.) I see.

Harjeet What the fuck is this?

Balbir (*rising*) Don't swear. I'll be in the conference room.

Harjeet Am I not privy to all internal affairs? Have you not stated that and made it general knowledge?

Balbir Yes.

Harjeet So this man – you Brains – where does he obtain the right to exclude me from confidences?

Balbir By my authority. You will be told what you need to know.

Harjeet 'Need to know'?

Balbir Yes.

Harjeet Oh this I like Uncle. After talk of absolute trust we discover its boundries.

Balbir What I give I take away. You must earn your way into my arms Harjeet.

Harjeet And here I stood thinking all the important things had been said.

Brains Listen, what you sayin' exactly?

Harjeet Take a pen, I'll spell it out.

Balbir Respect your elders Harjeet, those that have stood the test of time. (*He goes over and embraces him.*) Come here. Look at your face now! Where do you think my succession rests? You are the closest thing I have to a true son.

Harjeet Would you treat a son this way?

Balbir (*leaving*) The way it works in the old country is father to son. You have nothing to fear. I swear to you. Men like this will serve you one day. Now don't nick any pencils while I'm gone.

Harjeet *smiles and watches the two men leaving brushing off his rumpled clothes. He walks round the desk – looking in the drawers. Then he walks over to the picture of* **Balbir** *and the VIP and spits at it. He stands watching the spit trickle down the glass.*

Harjeet O how you stink of death. You stink of a whole world that's dead. What do you know of the modern ways?

He goes round and sits in **Balbir**'s *chair. He takes a manilla envelope from his inside pocket and puts it in the top drawer of the desk.*

Out with the old, in with the new. My eyes are burning to see what you can see. I want to look out over that vast expanse of . . . possibilities. No more brown tongueing you old Punjabi shit. The world will not wait.

The lights go up on the platform stage right. **Balbir** *and the* **Bodyguard** *are standing looking into a brown box. The* **Bodyguard** *is shaking visibly.* **Balbir** *turns to stare at the* **Henchmen**. *They look down.*

Bodyguard There was a phone call boss, then we found this. They said there are five more boxes. They said we could put him back together again. They laughed. Jesus Christ.

Balbir I am glad they have a sense of humour. (*Reaching into the box he takes out a decapitated head.*) He was a good chauffeur – for ten years. Look at his face. What would you call that expression? Terror or ecstacy? (**Balbir** *gently kisses the lips of the head.*)

Bodyguard Oh Christ boss, please.

The lights go down on platform stage right, and remain up on platform stage left. The television screen from the next scene turns on in the main stage area, it silently depicts images from Indian films – men fighting fantastic battles and overweight women singing to their lovers. **Harjeet** *is now sitting with his feet up on the desk. He has four pencils in his suit breast pocket, and is chewing on a fifth with a smile on his face. Suddenly* **Balbir** *enters and throws the turbanned decapitated head into his lap.*

Harjeet *screams and falls off the chair. He scrambles away from the vicinity of the head.*

Balbir (*shouting*) I've got the fear of God! What fuck shit do they think they're gonna scare!?

Balbir *takes out a flick-knife, he goes to where* **Harjeet** *is lying and pulls his head back by the hair. He holds the blade of the knife under his nose.*

I'll bite their bloody balls off!

Harjeet You mad bastard!

Balbir Yes maybe I am mad and rotted to the core. But have you known the love or sadness that I've known? Then what can you know of the hopes and desires that carried us?

He cuts a lock of hair from **Harjeet**'s *head.*

I've got God's fear. I have every species of fear. I have collected them and stored them away.

He sniffs the lock of hair as if it were a flower. **Harjeet** *goes and picks up the head.*

Harjeet Welcome to the new World, Uncle.

Scene 4

Manmohan *in his sitting room. Next to him he has a ceremonial sword and dagger. When the lights go up, he is sitting on the floor polishing the sword. A spotlight goes up on another part of the room, where sits the young* **Balbir** (*aged nine*) *on the floor. He is chewing a sugar cane.*

Balbir What you doing?

Manmohan *looks up.*

Went for a walk this morning. (*Indicating the sugar cane.*) Got one for you as well.

Manmohan Thank you Balbir.

Balbir Tha'ss O.K., you wan' it now?

Manmohan Yes please.

Balbir What you doing with that sword? Is it dad's sword?

Manmohan He gave it to me. Just now.

Balbir To keep?

Manmohan Yes.

Balbir You jammie bugger! What about me? I need one.

Pause.

What you gonna do with it then?

Pause.

Manmohan I'm going to cut my wrists.

Balbir Yeah! Really!?

Manmohan It's very sharp.

Balbir Great! You really gonna do it?

Manmohan Yes.

Balbir Great!

Manmohan Do you love me?

Balbir You what?

Manmohan I didn't understand anything. I followed without knowing. I accepted.

Balbir What?

Manmohan You.

Balbir Me?

Manmohan I never wanted anything.

Balbir Everyone does. I do.

Manmohan Just the sun on my back.

Balbir You get that anyway.

Manmohan No.

Balbir Will you still be my friend though?

Manmohan Yes.

Balbir Really! Always?

Manmohan Yes Balbir, always.

Scene 5

*On the platform, stage left, **Balbir**'s office. About twenty minutes after the events of Scene 2. **Balbir** stands facing the audience. He is reading the contents of the manilla envelope placed in his desk by **Harjeet**. **Harjeet** stands behind him, speaking over his shoulder. The **Bodyguard** stands some feet away, looking down at the floor.*

Harjeet They can call upon the loyalties of so many that would otherwise not dream of betrayal. An envelope in the desk. A contract. Just to let you know the turn of events. A gesture designed to inflict terror in the target. You cannot stem this particular tide. History, uncle. Looks to me like a radical rethink might be in order. These things escalate. Events acquire their own peculiar forces. A whirlpool commences at the point where the elements conjoin. That point which exerts the greatest gravitational attraction at a specific moment in time. We are all . . . sucked in. Eh, Brains, who's sucking you?

*A pause. He leans forward and licks the sweat from **Balbir**'s neck.*

You taste salty, uncle.

Scene 6

*Later in the evening. **Manmohan**'s sitting room. The video is on. He is lying on the floor, the Indian movie image fades and is replaced with **Balbir** in his present day form.*

Balbir's T.V Image Manmohan.

Manmohan Yes?

Balbir's T.V Image I left you alone. (*Pause.*) Forgive me, yaar.

Manmohan No.

Balbir's T.V Image What are you looking at?

Manmohan The stars in the sky. The moon and the sun. Every species of animal. Every insect and fish. The rivers of my life.

Balbir's T.V Image Can you see them all?

Manmohan Yes.

Balbir's T.V Image Then forgive.

Manmohan No.

*The video image fades. A white noise on the screen remains. After a while **Surinder** enters, having just returned from work. She comes in and steps over **Manmohan** knowing exactly where he is without having to look. The years have been fairly kind to **Surinder**, though she has grown heavier, but there is a sadness about her manner.*

Surinder (*taking off her overcoat*) Bloody buses. (*Going out with the coat. She enters after a moment.*) Bloody trains. (*She sits down.*) Bloody cancellations. (*She looks at the T.V screen for a moment, then gets up and turns it off.*) Bloody bastards. (*Pause.*) I'm not hungry. I'm dieting. Lose weight. that'll be good then. Lose weight. Be pretty again. Maybe that'll get me a better job. (*Pause.*) My tits hurt. (*Pause.*) There's a new young clerk in the office. I'll ask him to rub them for me. (*She laughs.*) I'll say it in front of everybody, I'll say, Peter file these away then give my tits a rub will you? You know what he'll do? He'll go and look in his job description. That's what they do nowadays. They look at their job descriptions. Maybe I'll stick it in as a trick; 'Item Seven, rub Office Manager's tits on request'. He'd do it then, if he saw it in black and white. He'd have to. (*Pause.*) You eat anything? Doesn't look like it. I can tell when you've eaten from how your belly sticks up. Are you holding it in? Trying to trick me? (*Pause.*) There's a mark on the carpet where you lie down. A light patch. You should move position sometimes to keep it even. (*Pause.*) You know what today is. Today is Wednesday. Exactly a week ago today it was last Wednesday. Amazing. You want to celebrate? (*Pause. She gets up.*)

Manmohan Surinder.

Surinder Hunjee.

Manmohan Lie down next to me.

Surinder Why?

Manmohan Just.

Surinder Oh no. Just because I mentioned my tits. This must be a new Manmohan. Is the carpet making you frisky, old man? Been watching pink videos?

Manmohan Blue videos.

Surinder What?

Manmohan They call them blue, not pink.

Surinder So, who cares what colour they are?

Manmohan Please, Surinder. Please lie down.

Surinder *hesitates then goes to sit next to him.*

Please.

Surinder *lies back.*

I still love you Surinder. I still love you.

Surinder (*after a pause*) How . . . how many years has it taken you to put together those words?

Pause.

Manmohan Look, you can see patterns through the clouds. The constellations. They never move in the sky. Nothing moves. Only we move. Nothing else moves.

Pause.

Surinder I would have been so much without you. Do you know that? The hopes I had.

Manmohan Will you always blame me?

Surinder I want to go home.

Manmohan This is home.

Surinder No, never.

Manmohan You know it's not the same back there.

Surinder I just want to be where I belong. My parents are still alive. I want to be near them.

Pause.

Manmohan But mine are dead.

Surinder Your land is rotting there, you know that? The land they fought so hard over?

Manmohan I know.

Surinder You can sell it. Get a plot. Build a house. (*Pause.*) But you won't will you? You'll let it rot till you die.

Manmohan Yes.

Surinder Every morning at work they say 'how are you?', every morning I say 'terrible, awful, never been worse'. They think it's a joke.

Manmohan I cannot make you happy Surinder.

Surinder *rolls over so that she is half on top of him – she rubs herself against him.*

Surinder This lying on the floor must wake the hormones up . . . You want to feel my hormones? (*Pause.*) Here or upstairs? Shall I pull your trousers down? You feel like it, eh?

Manmohan (*smiling at her*) No Surinder. I feel squashed.

She smiles and kisses him.

Surinder Isn't your wife a wonderful woman?

She kisses him again.

Scene 7

On the platform, stage left, **Balbir**'s *office.*
Harjeet, *the* **Bodyguard** *and the two*
Henchmen. *The* **Bodyguard** *is wiping*
blood from his mouth, **Harjeet** *hands him a*
clean hanky.

Harjeet What did the patronage of old
men do for you Brains? How, finally, did
your affections serve you? Did he take
you along? Are you with him Brains, or
here, left behind?

Bodyguard He'll be back I know it fer
sure. He'll turn this around on you.

Harjeet *expertly strikes him from behind. He*
falls to his knees. **Henchman 1** *loads a bullet*
into a gun which he then hands to **Harjeet.**

Harjeet Tell me Brains, do you think the
world works by chance and accident, or
can there be certainties?

He spins the barrel of the gun. The
Henchman *stand the* **Bodyguard** *up. They*
pull down his trousers and bend him over.
Harjeet *approaches and brutally shoves the*
gun into his anus.

Are you decided?

Bodyguard Jesus! Jesus Christ! Jesus
Christ!

Harjeet Sorry, is it too cold? Are you a
gambling man? I'd like to know. Where,
by the way, did he go to?

Bodyguard Fuck you!

We hear the click of the trigger being pulled.

No!

Harjeet Look at us here. Isn't this a
strange way to be? This is not ordinary
life. It's something higher and of greater
beauty. We can't fool around or take our
time.

Bodyguard Please! Oh holy Jesus!

Two more clicks in close succession. The
Bodyguard *falls forward,* **Harjeet** *topples*
with him. He bites into his ear. The

Bodyguard *shouts in pain.*

Harjeet There's pain in birth and so
there should be in death just to even the
score. We should despise mental peace
and freedom from anxiety. But this is no
way for a man to die. I loved my uncle to
some extent and cherish the things he
bred into me. I must see him one more
time and look into his face like a mirror.

Blackout.

Scene 8

Lights go up on the empty sitting room – later
that same night. **Balbir** *enters carrying a*
leather case. He is dressed very expensively in
a cashmere overcoat. He comes and looks
around the room as if he were in an art
gallery. He turns to watch **Manmohan** *enter*
slowly behind him. **Manmohan** *stands at the*
doorway and looks at **Balbir,** *a stunned*
expression on his face.

Balbir I've given you a surprise . . . I can
see I have (*Pause.*) This is a nice place.
Comfortable looking. (*Pause.*) You've
done it up nicely.

Manmohan How did you know . . . the
house?

Balbir That chair looks very cosy. (*Short*
pause. **Manmohan** *gestures for him to sit, but*
remains standing himself.) I didn't forget
you Manmohan. You thought I did, But I
couldn't. No. So I kept . . . I . . . I always
knew the basics of your life.

Manmohan Your lies haven't changed,
Balbir.

Balbir I knew where you lived . . . and
about the boy. (**Manmohan** *looks at him.*)
You chose a nice name for him.

Manmohan He's my son. I chose a name
for my son.

Balbir Yes, of course.

Manmohan We don't give a damn for it
you like it.

Balbir No, no. Why should you Manmohan.

Manmohan We don't want your opinions.

Balbir There's so much of you the same! (**Manmohan** *paces around the room, not looking at* **Balbir**.) I would have brought presents – yes – but I left in a rush. Business. You know. (*He starts to take out his wallet.*) So instead.

Manmohan Keep your money.

Balbir I just . . .

Manmohan Keep it.

Balbir Of course. If you like.

Manmohan Yes.

Balbir Ten, eleven hours in the Jag. Forty-eight without sleep. Can you see how my eyes are red? (**Manmohan** *looks at him.*) Yes I know they're red. (*Pause.*) I know what I did. It still burns me out. It still does.

Manmohan *slowly walks out of the room as* **Balbir** *speaks. A pause, then he storms back in again, speaking with anger and passion.*

Manmohan I've had a good life, a fine life!

Pause.

Balbir I just wanted a while with you. Just in the same room.

Manmohan Why?

Balbir On the way over, that's all I could think. I had to come, just to see you, hear your voice. To sit together. Like it was.

Manmohan To sit together.

Balbir Just a while with you. Maybe I'm a sentimental fool. I'm leaving the country – on business. Canada. It'll be a while. Probably a long time. I'll be moving around. So I wanted to see . . .

Manmohan . . . What you have done?

(*Clenching his fists.*) I should tear you to pieces.

Balbir *looks up at him. They stare.*
Manmohan *advances on him and grabs him.*
I should pull your heart out with my hands!

Balbir Maybe you should. Maybe the only way is to have my blood on your hands.

Manmohan What you did!

Balbir Understand me!

Manmohan (*pulling him up to his feet with his lapels*) I understand.

Balbir You helped me.

Manmohan No! Not you! I did nothing!

Balbir Without you I . . .

Manmohan (*pushing him forcefully into the chair*) I did nothing! Nothing! (*Pacing.*) Nothing! (**Manmohan** *throws himself against a wall and hits it with his fists.*) My son is a lawyer. He has achieved so much for himself . . .

Balbir He's a fine boy.

Manmohan *slowly slides to the floor during the next speech. He ends up in a sitting position, first facing the wall, then turning to look at* **Balbir** *with an expression of pain on his face.* **Balbir** *is trying to ignore the effect he is having.*

No one man can shape another life. I used to think it could be done. But my grasp . . . my grasp on certainly. My only quality, when I look back, was my certainty! The past twenty-eight years, none of them were not put to a specific purpose. Not one moment passed which wasn't like an arrow, pointed and flying towards it's mark. But you know . . . you know . . . mountains turn to dust, worlds explode, galaxies collapse. I'm not ashamed of anything that I've done. I look back with pride (*Pause.*) I like your carpet. (*Touching it.*) Quality. (*Pause.*)

How old is the wallpaper?

Manmohan Two years.

Balbir Yes.

Manmohan We put it up for Harjeet's wedding.

Balbir It's a nice girl he got there. A Scottish lassie.

Manmohan *looks at him.*

Balbir It's a nice pattern. I like the colours. You must have an eye for it.

Manmohan I just put it up.

Balbir a woman's touch eh? (*Pause.*) You weren't at the factory today?

Manmohan The factory closed down.

Balbir Oh.

Manmohan Sixteen months ago.

Balbir That long, sixteen months?

Manmohan They moved away. The whole thing.

Balbir They paid you though?

Manmohan Some money.

Balbir It's incumbent upon them.

Manmohan The union negotiated.

Balbir It's legally binding.

Manmohan That's what they told us. But the union . . .

Balbir They squeezed the best deal, eh?

Manmohan They got us more money.

Balbir Good. Make 'em do a useful job sometimes. The buggers, eh? The buggers. (*He laughs to himself.*)

Manmohan They got a lot more for us.

Balbir Even with the law. The law is an ass.

Manmohan Two, three thousand more.

Balbir You can't sniff at money, no

matter how little.

Manmohan We helped Harjeet.

Balbir Most parents wouldn't. Not anymore. I've seen that.

Manmohan With his house. The mortgage.

Balbir You remember how strong you were? Like a bullock. Strong like that. (*Pause.*) Like a bloody horse! Stand up again! Come on, take off your jacket. Let's see how you've gone, eh? (*Long pause.* **Manmohan** *does not move.*) I've carried guilt on my back Manmohan. (*Pause.*) I've carried your guilt.

Manmohan My guilt?

Balbir Why, I've never understood why you did it? (**Manmohan** *is uncomprehending.*) But I had to protect you.

Manmohan Protect me?

Balbir Yes.

Manmohan From what?

Balbir I had to. I did the right thing.

Manmohan What right thing?

Balbir The only woman I ever loved. You see the sacrifice I made? And you . . . it was you.

Manmohan No, no . . .

Balbir It's haunted me – what you did to her . . .

Manmohan No . . .

Balbir I know you thought you were saving me.

Manmohan Balbir . . . I didn't . . .

Balbir The way you . . . oh yes, that's what it was . . . what you did . . .Oh my god. Why, I've never understood why.

Manmohan Balbir, no!

Balbir That's why I had to run away. I

had to run away from you Manmohan.

Manmohan *is silent. He looks down into the palm of his right hand, rubbing it gently but obsessively.* **Balbir** *has buried his face in his hands.*

I would have had to tell Surinder. How you took my knife, you took my knife to do that thing.

Manmohan Balbir.

Balbir *looks at him.*

Balbir I loved her. My Jane. My poor Jane.

Manmohan I did not kill her.

Balbir (*angrily*) Why do you still deny it!? I saw you! I was there in the room! And then you took her body.

Manmohan Yes.

Balbir You took her away. Her poor dead body.

Manmohan Yes.

Balbir You hid her.

Manmohan Yes.

Balbir You killed her and hid her.

Manmohan No . . . I . . . no . . .

Balbir But I forgive you. You see, that's why I came back (*Pause.*) I truly forgive you.

Pause. **Manmohan** *is still rubbing his hand.*

Manmohan Thank you. Thank you . . .

Balbir I do . . . I do . . .

Manmohan Thank you . . .

They embrace.

Balbir All along I've been right. All along. (*Pause.*) You don't know how much you made me suffer. What you did to me. But, no, all that, it's all done with Hey! How about some tea.

Manmohan Tea?

Balbir (*elated*) Boy, oh boy. I remember your tea!

Manmohan (*getting up – still in a state of shock*) Yes. I'll make . . .

Balbir You don't know how good I feel. How good!

Manmohan You feel good?

Balbir (*jumping up*) Oh yes, yes, yes, yes! (*He goes over to kiss him.*) Let me give you a big hug!

Manmohan *holds* **Balbir** *back. Pause.*

Look, it's water, water under the bridge!

Manmohan Is it?

Balbir Of course!

Manmohan *turns and goes out.* **Balbir** *turns away from the door. He seems to have been imbued with a new lust for life. A weight truly has been lifted from his mind. He turns back to the door.*

Listen yaar, I'll kip in here if you don't object. So bloody knackered . . . forty-eight hours you know. Couple of times I fell asleep behind the wheel. Did half the trip with my eyes closed.

Manmohan *comes back in. He has not made any tea. He stands – desolate – looking at* **Balbir**.

Kee gul yaar, no tea bags?

Manmohan We have tea bags.

Balbir Actually, listen. Forget tea. Sod that. I'll kip down O.K. You carry on. I'll snuggle up in some corner.

Balbir *makes himself comfortable on the sofa. He gestures to* **Manmohan** *to put his overcoat over him, which* **Manmohan** *does. As the lights go down,* **Manmohan** *stands watching* **Balbir** *going to sleep. The lights go up on platform stage left,* **Balbir**'s *office. The* **Henchmen** *are packing some bags.* **Harjeet** *takes* **Balbir**'s *picture off the office wall, then he smashes it over the desk.*

Blackout

Scene 9

The living room, early next morning. **Balbir** *sits on the sofa, having just woken. He is re-arranging his hair and rubbing his eyes, giving a deep yawn. Enter* **Surinder**. *She stares at* **Balbir** *for a moment, then he sees her.*

Balbir My God! (*Pause.*) A visitation from heaven!

Surinder So this is our guest. I couldn't believe it when he told me.

Balbir It's wonderful. You don't know how happy this has made me!

Surinder You should be ashamed of yourself.

Balbir Sometimes I am.

Surinder Why don't you piss off.

Balbir Oh sister, you pain my soul! I love you both, my only family. I've come back!

Surinder We don't need you to come and shit all over us.

Balbir Angry words. Cruel words, sister. You were always hot in the temper, eh?

Surinder Why aren't you behind bars?

Balbir That is an extremely personal question. Where's my brother?

Surinder You've been disowned. Don't you know? Your adopted father renounced you years ago. Your name's pissed on by everyone. You've got no brother.

Balbir I think you'll find him in the kitchen cooking my breakfast.

Surinder You bastard.

Balbir You have more fat on you now. Not skinny like you were. (*He starts to put on his shoes and socks.*)

Surinder I know you inside out. Your kind.

Balbir A little knowledge can be lethal. You know? I know you also, my love. Oh yes.

Surinder What are you after? You want to be let off the hook after all this time? You want to come here with your sweet smiles and wipe the slate clean?

Balbir (*standing up*) Oh contraire! I came to forgive. (*He smiles.*) Yes.

Surinder (*after a pause*) I'd rather be blind than have to look at your face. We've got nothing to give a big man like you. Please just get in your Jaguar and drive away.

Balbir It's still the money thing that worries you isn't it, the loan I had to take? That I had every right to as it happens. (*He takes out a fat wallet.*)

Surinder You had no right to our money!

Balbir (*counting out some notes*) I had a . . . moral right. Without me that money would never had existed. Who do you think dragged him out here exactly? Without my foresight, you'd both still be shitting into a hole in the ground. (*He hands her the money.*)

Surinder (*taking the notes and calmly tearing them in two.*) Thanks very much.

Balbir You stupid bitch!

Surinder (*defiantly*) What are you going to do Balbir? Such a big man. So important.

Balbir (*closing in on her*) I'll fuck you up the arse. Re-kindle old flames.

Surinder *suddenly kicks him expertly in the testicles.* **Balbir** *keels over.*

Surinder You'll never get that close again.

Balbir I'll tear you open, you cunt. I'll tell your honest John husband the full facts. That'll educate him.

Surinder It was years ago.

Balbir You think so. Is that what he'll say?

Slight pause. **Manmohan** *enters with a tray upon which there are some plates of toast and eggs. He looks at* **Balbir**, *who is trying to stand up.*

I've got this sudden pain yaar.

Manmohan You want to see a doctor?

Balbir It comes and goes. I'll be fine.

Surinder Tell him to get out.

Balbir This is how you regard stricken relatives in this family, eh? My God! A fine situation!

Surinder We don't have to put up with him do we? There's no gain in it for us. Nothing.

Pause. **Manmohan** *studies both of them.*

Balbir I find this extraordinary!

Manmohan How long do you have to stay Balbir?

Balbir What perverse kind of question is that exactly?

Manmohan We . . . we both would like to know.

Balbir I travel all this way . . .

Surinder To laugh at us!

Balbir I was desperate in my heart to see you.

Manmohan I am a foolish man Balbir, my wife will tell you, but even I don't believe that.

Balbir You don't believe it because sometimes fact is stranger than fiction. After twenty eight years, the facts are incredible. Yes, even I won't believe them. But here I am! I'm at your mercy. You have your conscience . . . I know you have.

Manmohan . . . One more night. Just

tonight, then please never come back.

Balbir That's all I wanted. You are a fine man at heart. Men of your sort are filled with good will.

Surinder It's your house sure enough. If you can listen to all that without laughing in his face, you deserve all you get.

Balbir (*taking a slice of toast*) Look, I'll dash off to make my reservation, O.K? I have various pressing matters to attend to. You'll have time to resolve your differences and restore the glorious mantle of marital bliss, eh? (*He picks up his overcoat.*) I love you both. You cannot know how much I do! (*He goes and hugs* **Manmohan**, *is about to do the same to* **Surinder**, *but thinks better of it.*) My life is a circus!

Exits.

Surinder You've got the guts of a worm.

Manmohan Is this a matter of courage?

Surinder You call yourself a man? What is there 'manlike' about you?

Manmohan (*sitting down*) Nothing, perhaps.

Surinder You make me so ashamed. So sorry for the years we've wasted.

Manmohan You feel that way?

Surinder What do you expect?

Manmohan Meneoo nay patha. Menoo kushney patha.

Surinder Is that the truth? You know nothing? Have the years taught you nothing?

Manmohan What can I do? What words . . .

Surinder Look what's happened to my face. Look at me. I'm creased up with age!

Manmohan (*in an outburst*) What shall I

say to the father of my son!

Surinder Your son?

Manmohan I am not so stupid. Oh no. My eyes may be blank but they are not blind! (*Pause.*) I am a man . . . finally . . . I am a man . . . without dignity (*crying.*) Take out my eyes, cut out my tongue! (*Falling to hold her knees.*) Cut it out!

Surinder I . . .

Manmohan I am just a body. No soul. A dead man that twitches. What should a dead man do?

Surinder Manmohan, don't, stop now.

Manmohan I deserve everything.

Surinder No, no Manmohan.

Manmohan I know. I know Surinder.

Surinder Am I going mad? Tell me if I am, or tell me what you mean.

Manmohan Harjeet. Our Harjeet. My Harjeet. I know the truth.

Surinder What truth?

Manmohan I saw with these stupid eyes how he was made. I know he was never my son.

Pause.

Surinder You don't know anything. Even after all this.

Manmohan (*renewed sobbing*) No. No. No. He has taken everything.

Surinder That's right. He took everything that was yours.

Manmohan So he is, he is, my Harjeet . . . his son.

Surinder I don't know. I always believed in my heart he was yours. But there is no science to prove the beliefs of the heart. I don't know, and neither do you, neither does he. It was so long ago, Manmohan. (*Pause.*) At that moment, I would have let him do anything. (*He looks up at her.*) You brought him up as a son. Does it matter now?

Manmohan Yes.

Surinder It wouldn't change anything now.

Manmohan It would change . . .

Surinder No.

Manmohan It would change the past. The past.

Surinder No Manmohan, nothing can change the choices we made. (*Pause.*) Please, never tell Harjeet. We have no right . . .

Manmohan Do you think I could Surinder, could I look at him and tell him such things?

Pause. **Surinder** *stands looking at him.*

Surinder Manmohan. (*He does not look up.*) Manmohan.

She exits.

Pause then blackout.

Scene 10

On the Platform. Centre stage. The two **Henchman** *and* **Bodyguard** *stand in a triangle behind* **Harjeet**; *all dressed in black. The* **Henchmen** *carry bags.* **Harjeet** *is kneeling down caressing the wet ground with his hand. Flashing neon, as on a wet night.*

Harjeet I do not believe there's a God or logic to the world. No fate or price to pay. I'm an optimist, and I think things will turn out right. As long as there's money. As long as there are cars worth driving and girls worth fucking.

Henchman 'Tis a big city boss. The big smoke.

Henchman II People like rats. Running around.

Harjeet Am I right or wrong? Where do

words take us?

The **Bodyguard** *leans forward and, putting his hands under* **Harjeet***'s armpits, lifts him up.* **Harjeet** *is like a rag doll – his legs slightly bent, his body and neck limp.*

We're heathens then, apostates. We've spat at the gods.

They all spit in different directions.

And they must spit back.

Blackout.

Scene 11

Enter **Manmohan** *looking downcast, followed by* **Balbir***, who is in good spirits.*

Balbir They managed to put me on a flight going out tonight. First class. I won't have to exploit your hospitality a minute more. (*Pause.*) I should be sad, but I'm not. Perhaps a tear or two. Perhaps. But well – we move on, we move ahead. I . . . I am escaping my fate.

Manmohan I don't understand you.

Balbir You never did. You think I forgot you. I didn't forget. No. Ask your son. Ask him.

Manmohan You betrayed . . .

Balbir Ah, ah, ah. Come on now. We're beyond all that. Don't talk in relative terms. You'll never see me again, so let sleeping dogs lie. Forget.

Manmohan No. You can't brush me away. I'm in your head!

Balbir Are you? Are you?

Manmohan I hate you Balbir.

Balbir Hate? Good.

Manmohan I hate you!

Balbir You've always hated me.

Manmohan No!

Balbir Always. But you were too scared. You were afraid Manmohan.

Manmohan, *in a rage, picks up the television set and hurls it to the ground.* **Balbir** *is unperturbed. They look at each other. A pause.*

Good. Release your spirits, the wicked ones. I want to say goodbye to Surinder. (*Pause.*) Where is she, eh? (*Turning to the doorway.*) Sulky business I will not stand. No, sir.

Manmohan *advances on him. He grabs him and pulls him slowly towards the centre of the room. They stand –* **Manmohan** *holding his brother by the wrists, grim determination in his eyes.*

Manmohan She's gone.

Balbir Where?

Manmohan Away.

Balbir Well . . . I should have taught you long ago . . . about women . . .

Manmohan What. What about them?

Balbir Bitches. You know. Bitches.

Manmohan Like the one I killed?

Balbir You killed?

Manmohan The one I did.

Balbir Yes. Like that. Like that.

Manmohan Jane.

Balbir Yes, Jane.

Manmohan *suddenly grabs* **Balbir** *by the throat and starts to strangle him.* **Balbir** *also grabs* **Manmohan** *'s throat, but is unable to match his strength – he then tries to pull away his hands, but cannot. They are frozen like this,* **Manmohan** *in grim determination, and* **Balbir** *with the look of a drowning man.* **Harjeet**, *two* **Henchmen** *and the* **Bodyguard** *enter – the* **Bodyguard** *carries a shotgun. They stand watching for a moment.* **Balbir**, *choking, starts to sink to the ground.*

Harjeet Let him go Dad.

Looking up, **Manmohan** *loosens his grip.*

Please dad, let him go.

Manmohan lets go.

Thank you Dad.

Balbir *scrambles over to* **Harjeet** *and grabs his legs.* **Harjeet** *takes the shotgun from the* **Bodyguard**.

Harjeet Uncle, you seem to me like a desperate man. Let me look at you.

Balbir *looks up. He is crying.*

Balbir Is it the Gods? Is it? What is it that makes a man?

Harjeet I know not uncle. 'Tis academic now. The professors will fret.

Pause. He looks at one of the **Henchman**.

First Henchman The collision of events?

Harjeet Perhaps. (*Pause.*) He's been good t'me dad, he should've hold you.

Manmohan Harjeet.

Harjeet He should've told you.

He looks down at **Balbir** *then, pointing the shotgun into his face, fires.*

Blackout.

Scene 12

Possibly on the Platform, (but preferably on the main playing area), centre stage. A clear Indian night. Blustery. The sound of wailing women which dies into the background. The same field where the play began. **Manmohan** *has built a funeral pyre upon which lies the shrouded body of* **Balbir**. *He stands looking up with a burning torch in his hand.*

Manmohan This is the field, my brother, my blood, where we sat and played and made our life-long promises. This the field where you planted the seed for a money tree to grow. It grew into our hearts my brother. (*Pause.*) It poisoned our blood. (*Pause.*) I will scatter your sacred ashes in the river. You will nourish the soil . . . (*Slowly.*) . . . I loved you . . .

He puts the torch to the pyre. Lights go down.